domain.456

Families
The Environment
Sports & Competition

Bev Gundersen and Linda Kondracki

Cook Ministry Resources
a division of Cook Communications Ministries
Colorado Springs, Colorado/Paris, Ontario

domain.456: Families, The Environment, Sports & Competition

© 1991, 1998 David C. Cook Church Ministries

All rights reserved. Except for the reproducible Activity Sheets, which may be copied for classroom use, and the newsletter *PARTNERS*, which may be copied for distribution to parents, no part of this book may be reproduced or used in any form without the written permission of the publisher, unless otherwise noted in the text.

Scripture quotations are from the Holy Bible: New International Version (NIV), © 1973, 1978, 1984 by the International Bible Society. Used by permission of Zondervan Bible Publishers.

Published by Cook Ministry Resources
4050 Lee Vance View
Colorado Springs, CO 80918-7100
www.cookministries.com

Designed by Jeff Jansen
Illustrated by Sonny Carder
Printed in U.S.A.

ISBN: 0-7814-5514-6

Table of Contents

   4 **Welcome to the Junior Electives Series**

Families

   6 **Overview**
   9 **Lesson 1**
      Gifts from God (Family Members Are Gifts)
  17 **Lesson 2**
      Family Daze (Handling Family Changes)
  25 **Lesson 3**
      I've Got a Secret (Abuse in the Family)
  33 **Lesson 4**
      It Runs in the Family (Caring for One Another in My Family)
  41 **Lesson 5**
      Part of the Family of God (Belonging to God's Family)
  49 **Families Unit Service Projects**

The Environment

  50 **Overview**
  53 **Lesson 1**
      Our Unique Planet (Our Specially Created World)
  61 **Lesson 2**
      A World Full of Wonder (A Creative God)
  69 **Lesson 3**
      Caretakers of Earth (Our God-appointed Role as Stewards of Our World)
  77 **Lesson 4**
      United, We Save (What Can We Do to Save the Earth?)
  85 **The Environment Unit Service Projects**

Sports and Competition

  86 **Overview**
  89 **Lesson 1**
      God and My Bod (Using the Body and Mind God Gave Me)
  97 **Lesson 2**
      Fair Play (Being Fair)
105 **Lesson 3**
      It's How You Play the Game (Winning and Losing)
113 **Lesson 4**
      Go Team, Go! (Teamwork and Cooperation)
121 **Sports and Competition Unit Service Projects**

✓ Junior Electives

Welcome to the Junior Electives Series

✓ Let's talk about it . . .

What is it like to grow up in America today? How do our Junior-age children perceive the world around them, and their place in it? Did you know that your Junior students are more aware of the world around them than any previous generation of American children? However, seen through their eyes the world is often seen as a scary and anxious place. Every day they are blatantly confronted with the threat of nuclear disasters, ecological concerns that warn them their planet may not exist by the time they grow up, and an increasing number of their classmates either wielding knives and guns at school or killed in gang-related incidents. Closer to home, you can expect a high number of your students to have experienced at least one divorce in their family, or suffered some kind of physical, sexual, or emotional abuse from family members.

As adults, we may like to close our eyes and see the days of childhood as carefree and innocent as they might have been in our day. But when we open our eyes and see the world as our kids see it today, it is clear that life holds much stress and anxiety for our children. Instead of wishing for simpler days, it is time for us to say to our kids, "Let's talk about it . . ."

The Junior Electives Series was designed to help you do just that. Each topic in the series was selected because it represents issues Juniors are concerned about, and in many cases learning about from their peers, the media, or in school. With the help of this curriculum, you will be able to provide an opportunity for them to discuss their concerns in a Christian context. For many of your kids, this may be the first chance they will have to hear that the Bible has a lot to teach them about each of these contemporary life concerns.

As you teach the lessons in this series, you will have an opportunity to:
• Introduce and teach topics of concern to Juniors in a distinctively Christian context.
• Provide a safe place to learn about, talk about, and express feelings about each issue.
• Teach practical skills and biblical principles Juniors can use to cope with each concern in their daily lives.
• Provide a tool to help parents facilitate family discussion and coping in the home setting.

✓ Features of the Junior Elective Series

Four-Part Lesson Plan

Each lesson follows this format:

1. Setting the Stage (5-10 minutes). Each lesson begins with an activity designed to do two things. First, it is a gathering activity, meaning that you can involve your students in it as soon as they arrive. You do *not* need to have the whole class present to begin your lesson time. By arriving early and having the Setting the Stage activity set up and ready for the kids as soon as they walk in the door, you will communicate a sense of excitement about the lesson and set a tone of orderliness for your class.

Second, the Setting the Stage activity is purposeful in that it will draw the students into the subject for the day. It is more than just something to keep the kids busy while everyone arrives. The activity will provide a fun and interesting way to draw the kids' attention to an area of interest in their lives. Most of the time, it will also raise questions which will lead them into the next section of the lesson.

2. Introducing the Issue (20 minutes). Building on the Setting the Stage activity, this section of the lesson will involve the kids in an active discussion of the topic of the day. The material provided for you contains information the kids need to know, anticipating key questions they may have. It also includes one or more learning activities particularly designed to encourage your students to talk about the issues most on their minds, while in the context of a Christian community. To make this time as effective as possible, you will need to establish your class as a safe place where everyone's feelings and questions are welcomed and treated seriously (some suggestions for doing that are listed on page 5). Once that has been accomplished, you may be surprised at how much your Juniors have to say, and the depth of their thinking!

3. Searching the Scriptures (20 minutes). This section of each lesson takes your class to the Bible to discover what God has to say about the topic being discussed. Your students may be amazed to find out just how much the Bible says about subjects that seem so *modern*. Through a wide variety of creative teaching methods, your class will study people and principles of Scripture that speak directly to the concerns gripping their hearts and minds. As you study together, you will also be acquainting them with the most valuable resource they can have for coping with these contemporary issues: their Bibles.

4. Living the Lesson (5-10 minutes). The final section of each lesson challenges the kids to take what they've learned and apply it to their own lives. It's the *so what* section. The class members will be encouraged to ask themselves, "So what am I going to do with what I've just learned?"

Clearly Stated Key Principles

Each book in the Junior Electives Series contains three units, each of which addresses a different topic of concern. The following three unit features will help your students focus on and remember the central principles of each unit.

1. Unit Verse. One verse has been chosen for each unit that summarizes the biblical principle central to the unit topic. The meaning of this verse is developed a little more each week as students work on a cooperative learning activity designed to help them understand and apply a key biblical principle.

2. Unit Affirmation. The primary learning objective for each unit has been phrased into an affirmation sentence that begins with "I can . . . " Discussing this affirmation each week will empower your students by letting them know they can do something positive about issues that may feel frightening or overwhelming.

3. Unit Service Projects. At the end of each unit you will find several ideas for your class not only to learn about the unit issue, but actually DO something about it. Although they are optional, taking the extra time to involve your class in a unit project will help them practice new skills and see for themselves that they can take an active role in the issues that affect their lives.

Parent Informational Letter

At the beginning of each unit, you will find PARTNERS . . . , a newsletter that you can photocopy and send home to the parents of your class members. This letter gives parents an overview of the topic being studied, as well as some practical ideas of ways they can further their child's learning through several Do-At-Home activities.

Flexibility and Variety

The Junior Electives Series has been designed to be usable in any number of settings. It is equally effective in a Sunday-school setting, a Wednesday-night series, or even a special setting such as a weekend retreat. If you live in an area that participates in release time, this series is an exellent resource to present biblical principles in a contemporary way. Feel free to be creative and find the best place for your group to talk about these important life principles.

A variety of learning activities are used to present the issue information and biblical truths. The following materials are considered standard supplies and are recommended to be available for the classtimes:

- Bibles
- Glue
- Tape
- Pencils
- Scissors
- Stapler
- Paper

A Word about Children and Stress . . .

As you prepare to teach the Junior Electives Series, it is important to realize that many of the subjects you will be studying are the sources of stress in the lives of your students. Many students may never have had the chance to talk openly about these issues, and doing so in your class may well raise their anxiety level. Throughout these sessions, there are several things you can keep in mind:

1) Point them to Jesus. Perhaps the greatest benefit of the Junior Elective Series is that it will give you the opportunity to help your kids learn that a relationship to Jesus Christ is the best resource we can have to face the stressful, anxious parts of our lives. Through the Bible studies and your own personal witness of the power of Christ in your life, you can have the privilege of introducing children to Jesus and inviting them to ask Him to be an active part of their lives.

2) Create a safe place where they can talk about their real feelings. Children have a strong tendency to say the things in class that they think teachers want to hear. Early on in this series, you will want to create a safe place for sharing by continually reassuring your kids that they can say what is really on their minds, and making a rule that no one can criticize or make fun of anything anyone else shares in class. In many cases, expressing their feelings in a safe place, and having those feelings accepted by you and the class will relieve much of their anxiety.

3) If necessary, help them get outside help. You may find a child in your class who is experiencing an unusual amount of stress. In that case, ask your pastor or Christian Education Director for the procedure your church uses to refer children and families for professional help.

Families

It's All in the Family...

The word "family" has a very different meaning today than it did not much more than ten years ago. It used to be that "family" meant two parents and their children all living together, often with the father being the provider and the mother the homemaker. Today, fewer children live in that kind of family. No doubt in your class of Juniors you have some kids who live in single-parent homes or step-families, or at least one child who is living in an abusive situation. In America today, many millions of our children are experiencing great stress in the setting that God intended to be the source of love, security, and teaching about life. Even children who live in two parent families are often anxious about the possibility of a divorce happening in their families, and those who have experienced divorce or abuse struggle to cope with their situations.

This unit will address some of these issues, giving your students a safe place to talk about any concerns they may have about their families. It will also present a positive perspective by reassuring them that there are no perfect families and that they can enjoy living in their families when they learn that everyone has to work hard to make a family special. You will also have an opportunity to share with them the privilege they have to belong to God's family, and show them how they can respond to God's invitation to do so.

Families Overview

Unit Verse: I will be a Father to you, and you will be my sons and daughters, says the Lord Almighty. II Corinthians 6:18

Unit Affirmation: I CAN ENJOY LIVING IN MY FAMILY!

LESSON	TITLE	OBJECTIVE	SCRIPTURE BASE
Lesson #1	Gifts from God	That your students will show their appreciation to family members and acknowledge them as God's gifts.	I Samuel 1:1, 2, 9-11, 20-28
Lesson #2	Family Daze	That your students will seek God's help to handle changes in their families.	Ruth 1:1-18
Lesson #3	I've Got a Secret	That your students will seek out God and also wise people who can help them when they suffer abuse in their families.	Matthew 18:1-7
Lesson #4	It Runs in the Family	That your students will commit themselves to caring for people in their families.	I Corinthians 13:4-7
Lesson #5	Part of the Family of God	That your students will choose to follow Jesus and become part of God's family.	Galatians 4:4-7

Partners

Keeping Parents Informed and Involved!

For the next few weeks your Junior-age child will be part of a group learning about Families. *Partners* is a planned parent piece to keep you informed of what will be taught during this exciting series.

PREVIEW...

Family Life

The word "family" has taken on a whole new meaning in the past few decades. Not so long ago, "family" meant two parents and their children all living together, often with the father being the provider and the mother the homemaker. Today, fewer families fit that picture. Factors such as a high divorce rate, blended families, and a new awareness of family violence leaves us searching for new definitions of what family is all about.

The truth remains, however, that family is still the most significant place of belonging and caring for our children. As parents, the job of making family a safe, loving place for children to grow up is still our primary responsibility. However, that task is becoming more difficult as our society forces kids to grow up too fast, and parents are often consumed with handling the stresses in their own lives.

In the next few weeks, your kids will have the opportunity to talk about what it means to be family. This unit is designed to encourage them by affirming the special gift that our families are to us. They will also discover that they can belong to more than one family, as they are invited to respond to God's invitation for them to become members of His family. These concepts will be reinforced each week as they review the following:

Unit Verse:

I will be a Father to you, and you will be my sons and daughters, says the Lord Almighty.
II Corinthians 6:18

Unit Affirmation:

I CAN ENJOY LIVING IN MY FAMILY!

PRINCIPLES...

Family Life
PRINCIPLE #1:

THERE ARE NO PERFECT FAMILIES. Junior-age kids are just beginning to see the imperfections in their own families and compare their families to others. (You may be sick of hearing how terrific life is in the family of your child's best friend!) As a parent, it can help to know that this is normal developmental behavior for this age group. Especially in families where there has been some kind of disruption, kids can feel that their family is not a family anymore, and wish they lived in a "real" family. Children deal with the imperfections in many different ways. Some may become verbally critical of their home life, which is particularly hard for parents to deal with! Others handle it in their imaginations, wishing they lived somewhere else, or even making up their ideal family and pretending they live there.

This unit will address these issues by assuring kids that although it can be hard to come to terms with the imperfections in their families, there is a way to deal with it. The next two principles explain this further.

PRINCIPLE #2:

WE HAVE TO WORK HARD AT BEING GOOD FAMILIES. When we watch television a lot, we can get the message that "normal" families do not have to work hard at being strong and healthy. The truth is that healthy families work hard at "being family" together. The first key to making our families work is having

©1991 David C. Cook Publishing Co. Permission granted to reproduce for distribution to parents only.

Partners

an active commitment to each other. Unfortunately, in our society today your kids are receiving few models of what it means to be committed to anything.

In this unit, they will learn that being committed means caring for each other's needs, and caring for each others needs means that we know what other's need and want from us. We take the time to listen and do things for others and make the effort to care for them even when it is inconvenient or hard for us to do so!

PRINCIPLE #3:

GOD INVITES US TO JOIN HIS FAMILY. Because we live in imperfect families, it is also important to understand that no matter how committed we may be to each other, there will always be times when our families cannot meet our needs. In a very special lesson in this unit, your kids will learn that there is a family with a loving Father who wants to adopt us and take care of us. This family also has lots of people in it who care for one another in special ways. That Father is God, and His family is the church. We can belong to God's family at the same time we belong to our own family. In fact, we very much need both families.

Responding to God's invitation to join His family is one of the most important aspects of our life on earth. When we do, God promises to be with us always, teaches us the best way to live, and provides the church family as a caring community to help us through whatever life may bring. And, best of all, there are no permanent good-byes in God's

family. We will be with our loving Father and His family throughout all eternity!

PRACTICE...

Family Life

1. EXPLORE THE MEANING OF COMMITMENT.

One of the activities your child will do in class during this unit is to make an acrostic using the word "Commitment." Repeating this activity at home can help you have a significant conversation with all family members regarding the commitment you want to make to each other. For your discussion, start with a piece of poster board with the word "Commitment" written vertically down the left-hand side. Then decide as a family which statements you would like to list as an example of your commitment to each other. The following is an example of how to make an acrostic, but you must come up with your own statements:

C- are for each other
O- bey parents without complaining
M- ake time for each other
M- ention good things
 I - nquire about each other's activities and interests
T- ake time to listen
M- end hurts
E- xtend sympathy to those who hurt
N- o unkind comments!
T- hink about the needs of others

2. CELEBRATE YOUR FAMILY.

Plan a specific night to focus on how special your family is. Enjoy a favorite family meal, and then spend time looking through family photo albums and mementos. Enjoy remembering the good times, and grieve together over past losses and changes. Then, encourage your kids to ask you any questions about your life growing up, or the lives of grandparents, other relatives, and family friends. As they listen to these stories, they will gain a sense of connectedness which is an essential ingredient to strong family life. (This is also true for adoptive and step-families.)

3. BELONGING TO GOD'S FAMILY.

One of the greatest resources God gives us is His family on earth, the church family. Be sure you are connected to your church in ways that will enable you to receive the most benefits from it. This includes regular attendance at worship services, belonging to a small group who knows you well and can pray with and for you, and being sure your children have significant friendships with other church families. You might even make a COMMITMENT poster to summarize your relationship to your church family. Remember, both your families are gifts from God to you!

Families

Gifts from God

Aim: That your students will show their appreciation to family members and acknowledge them as God's gifts
Scripture: I Samuel 1:1, 2, 9-11, 20-28
Unit Verse: I will be a Father to you, and you will be my sons and daughters, says the Lord Almighty. II Corinthians 6:18
Unit Affirmation: I CAN ENJOY LIVING IN MY FAMILY!

 **Planning Ahead**

1. Photocopy Activity Sheets (pages 15 and 16)—one for each student.
2. Gather several resource books with specific information about animal families for SETTING THE STAGE. Suggested animals: turtles, eagles, wolves, deer. Choose a minimum of three different animals, and at least one animal per five kids.
3. Set up centers as described in SETTING THE STAGE.
4. Prepare the Unit Affirmation poster by writing across the top of a large poster board: I CAN ENJOY LIVING IN MY FAMILY! Under the title, write the numbers 1-5 vertically down the left-hand side.

 Setting the Stage (5-10 minutes)
WHAT YOU'LL DO
- Research characteristics of animal families

WHAT YOU'LL NEED
- Resource books about families of animals

 Introducing the Issue (20 minutes)
WHAT YOU'LL DO
- Discuss reasons we have families
- Make a "Family Gallery" to discover the uniqueness of each family
- Use an activity sheet to discuss the importance of commitment to successful family life
- Introduce the Unit Affirmation poster

WHAT YOU'LL NEED
- "Key in to Family Life!" Activity Sheet (page 15)
- Unit Affirmation poster

 Searching the Scriptures (20 minutes)
WHAT YOU'LL DO
- Draw a "photo" album Hannah might have made to learn how family members are God's gifts to each other

WHAT YOU'LL NEED
- Bibles
- Red construction paper—one sheet for each student, scissors

 Living the Lesson (5-10 minutes)
WHAT YOU'LL DO
- Use an activity sheet to brainstorm ideas about ways to show appreciation to family members then complete gift tags for those members

WHAT YOU'LL NEED
- "Two-Way Gifts" Activity Sheet (page 16)

 # Lesson 1 — Families

 ## Setting the Stage (5-10 minutes)

Before your students arrive today, set up centers around the room (a minimum of three centers and at least one center per five kids). At each center, place a resource book opened to the pages describing the animal the kids will research at that table, paper and markers. As kids arrive, direct them to one of the centers and instruct them to use the materials to find the following information about the family life of that center's animal. They can use pictures and words to present information about 1) how the young are born, 2) how involved they are with the parents and siblings, and 3) how long the "children" stay in the family. Ask each group to share its findings with the rest of the class. **What are the differences in the families we have just heard about?** The differences will range from turtles that lay their eggs and never even see their young, to wolves with a relatively sophisticated community life. **Today we are beginning a unit about living in our families—something we often take for granted. But just as God designed the way each of the animal families would work, He also designed our families to do certain things for us. In the next few weeks, we will talk about God's plan for our families.**

 ## Introducing the Issue (20 minutes)

What are some of the differences between animal families and our families? Point out differences such as human babies are more dependent on their families and need more care than most animals, humans have a life-time connection to their families, humans have a sense of history (animals know nothing of grandparents and ancestors), humans often make plans for and anticipate the joy of having children. **Placing us in a family is God's way of taking care of us. What do our families actually do for us?** Write responses on the board as kids suggest them. Items to include: provide physical needs of food and shelter, keep us safe, teach us how to care for ourselves (humans have very low natural instincts compared to animals; kids have to be taught the skills of survival), talk and listen to us. **What do kids do for families?** In most cases, kids bring love, joy, and laughter to families, they also keep the family going as they grow and have children of their own.

Invite your kids to introduce their families to each other by making a "Family Gallery." Distribute paper and markers and instruct your students to draw family houses that depict their homes and all the people who live there. If they live in two houses, they can divide their paper in half and draw both homes.

Families

Lesson 1

In the margins, they can draw other important family members such as grandparents. When the pictures are done, they can share them with each other and attach them to the wall to make a "Family Gallery" around your room.

As you can see, all of our families are different. Every one of them is special and unique, no matter how many or few people may be in it. What are some things that make your family special and unique? Give kids an opportunity to respond. Ideas might be things they like to do together, a relative that lives in Alaska or a foreign country, a special holiday tradition, etc. **We must also remember that none of our families is perfect. We all have things we wish were different about our families and things that could be better. What are some things that you wish could be different about your family?** Give kids an opportunity to share their feelings about this subject. **During those times when our families are not quite what we wish they could be, it is important to remember that no matter what, they are still an important gift to us. We can value them, and be committed to them as our most important place of belonging.**

Distribute copies of the activity sheet, "Key in to Family Life" (page 15), and look at it together. **Commitment is an important quality we don't talk about very often. But it is the key to make any relationship work well, especially relationships within our families.** Guide your students to think about the meaning of commitment within families by making an acrostic. Think of characteristics or examples of family commitment that begin with the letters in the key and write them on the lines. The following is one possible acrostic. Your kids can think of other possibilities for theirs.

C - Care for each other
O - Obey parents without complaining
M - Make time for each other
M - Mention good things
I - Inquire about each other's activities and interests
T - Take time to listen
M - Mend hurts
E - Extend sympathy to those who hurt
N - No unkind comments!
T - Think about the needs of others

These things are not always easy to do. Being committed to each other is hard work! But that's what commitment means: working hard to help make our families good places to live for all family members!

Display the Unit Affirmation poster and read it aloud together as a class. Each week during the unit you will be adding a phrase that captures the theme of the week's lesson and further helps to explain the meaning of the

Families

affirmation. **Let's think about what we learned today that can help us live happily in our families.** Let kids suggest phrases. One possibility would be "by being committed to everyone in it!" Choose one phrase and write it on the first line. **Now let's look at a Bible story about one very special family.**

 # Searching the Scriptures (20 minutes)

Let's turn to I Samuel chapter one and see how God gave some family members to each other in a very special way. Because verses one and two have several difficult names, read them aloud to your students.

Have kids take turns reading verses 9-11. **According to these verses how do you think Hannah was feeling?** (Miserable, bitter, sad, lonely.) Verses 12 and 13 seem to indicate that even Eli, God's high priest, misunderstood her and the depth of her misery. Junior-age kids are on the brink of being teenagers. They do, or will have, many of the same feelings Hannah experienced. They need the love and support of family members. **Have you ever felt something like Hannah did? What did you do about it?** Let kids share briefly.

Ask someone to read Psalm 68:6 aloud. **What is one reason God gives us families?** (So we won't be lonely.) **How do you think this verse would have made Hannah feel?** (Good.) **How does it make you feel?** Although we sometimes get upset with our family and wish we had some time alone, it usually doesn't take very long before we miss them and long for them again.

What made Hannah feel so miserable? (She had no children.) **What did she do about her problem?** (Prayed to the Lord and asked Him to give her a son.) **Hannah knew where to go to find help and encouragement. She understood that God is the one who gives us our families and she trusted Him to answer her prayer. What promise did Hannah make to the Lord, if He would give her a son?** (She would give him back to the Lord to serve Him all his life.)

Have students take turns reading verses 20-28. **Hannah named her baby boy Samuel. Why did she name him that?** Samuel means "heard of God." She named him this because she recognized God had heard her prayer and answered it with this special gift. Hannah was thankful to God for the baby boy He had given her. We need to be thankful to God for our families too. When we show our appreciation to members of our families, we make God happy and honor Him.

Samuel's parents loved and followed God. What was his family like? Elkanah had two wives, something that often occurred in the time of the Old Testament. One of these wives was constantly putting down Hannah, the other

Families Lesson 1

wife, Samuel's mother. From the words of verse eight we can assume that Elkanah didn't totally understand Hannah's feelings. However, he loved Hannah very much. He respected her promise to God and agreed to follow through on it with her. **How is this family like our families?** There are no perfect families. Families are not always as we would like them to be because they are made up of people who are imperfect, but they are still the people whom God has given to you to love and care for you. Working together for God is a great blessing to us and others.

Check out verse 28. What did Hannah do with Samuel? (She gave him back to the Lord to live at the temple and serve God there all his life.) He was only about three years old when Hannah took him to Eli. Samuel grew up without the benefit of the daily physical love and care of his parents.

How do you think Hannah and Elkanah felt about leaving Samuel and going home alone? Stress that although they were lonesome for their little boy they were also happy. Hannah's song of praise in chapter two is a beautiful expression of praise and joy from a mother who knows God is in control of everything, including her family. She gave the Lord her dearest possession, her son, and trusted Him to watch over Samuel faithfully.

Even though she was not near Samuel, Hannah didn't forget about him. Have someone read I Samuel 2:19. **What did she do for Samuel?** (Each year she made him a robe and took it to him.) Hannah was a woman of prayer as we have already seen and we can be sure she prayed for her son constantly. When Samuel grew up and was a judge, he lived in his parents' hometown of Ramah. Perhaps this was so he could be near his family.

Distribute paper and drawing materials. Have students fold their paper in half lengthwise and crosswise to make four sections. Explain that kids will draw a "photo album" of pictures and comments Hannah might have made about Samuel. They can use simple stick-figure drawings. Pictures might show her praying at Shiloh, holding baby Samuel, presenting him to Eli at the temple, and praying for her growing son or taking him a new coat. Statements can be brief and should be a commentary on the pictures.

Allow time to complete this activity.

Samuel was only a little boy when Hannah took him to the temple to be God's servant. He only saw his parents once a year

13

Lesson 1 — Families

when they came to worship God there. How do you think he felt as he was growing up in the temple? (Lonely, glad to see his parents when they came.) Have students turn to the Unit Verse which is found in II Corinthians 6:18 and read it together. **How do you think Samuel would have felt about this verse?** (Happy, less lonely, comforted, loved, close to God.) **How do you feel about this verse?** Let students share briefly. Be sensitive to kids who appear to be lonely or sad. Make it a point to try to get to know them better and visit them in their homes. **God has given our family members to us. He wants us to love and appreciate them as His special gifts.**

Distribute the construction paper and scissors. Have kids cut a large heart the size of the sheet. While they are doing this, explain the Unit Verse activity. **Although no family is perfect, you will have the opportunity to design your "Ideal Family" during this unit.** Explain that an "Ideal Family" is what a kid would have if he or she could have a family exactly like she or he wished. Have kids write their names on the heart, then number from one to five along the left side of the heart, leaving spaces between the numbers to write something each week. Next to number one they can write the names of people they would like to have as members of their "Ideal Family." Keep all the hearts in the classroom to be used next week.

✔ Living the Lesson (5-10 minutes)

All our family members, brothers, sisters, mom, dad, and extended family are one-of-a-kind creations and special gifts to us from God. What are some ways we can show our appreciation to them? Spend two to three minutes brainstorming ways. Some suggestions are: phoning or writing a postcard expressing love, asking about and listening to them, complimenting or bragging about something good they've done or how special they are, giving them some favorite small item such as a magazine or treat, playing their favorite game.

Distribute copies of the activity sheet "Two-Way Gifts" (page 16). Invite kids to share their appreciation ideas with the group and then complete the gift tags.

Encourage students to close in prayer, thanking God for their families.

Key in to Family Life!

Our families are gifts from God to us. But living in our families can sometimes be hard. Families work best only when all the members are willing to work hard and be committed to each other.

On each line below, write a characteristic or example of what it means for family members to be committed to each other. Start each characteristic with the same letter as is in the key. The first one is done to get you started.

C are for each other
O _____
M _____
M _____
I _____
T _____
M _____
E _____
N _____
T _____

Activity Sheet by Linda Kondracki © 1991 David C. Cook Publishing Co. Permission granted to reproduce for classroom use only.

✓  Two-Way Gifts

God has given your family members to you as a gift. What can you do so they will know you are glad that God chose them as a gift for you?

Make a gift tag and give it to someone in your family. In the space beside "TO" write a family member's name. Fill in your name and then write something you can do to show your appreciation to that person.

To:

You are a gift from God to Me.

I can show my appreciation by:

_____
_____
_____
_____
_____

To:

You are a gift from God to Me.

I can show my appreciation by:

_____
_____
_____
_____
_____

To:

You are a gift from God to Me.

I can show my appreciation by:

_____
_____
_____
_____
_____

To:

You are a gift from God to Me.

I can show my appreciation by:

_____
_____
_____
_____
_____

Activity Sheet by Bev Gundersen © 1991 David C. Cook Publishing Co. Permission granted to reproduce for classroom use only.

Families

Lesson 2

Family Daze

Aim: That your students will seek God's help to handle changes in their families
Scripture: Ruth 1:1-18
Unit Verse: I will be a Father to you, and you will be my sons and daughters, says the Lord Almighty. II Corinthians 6:18
Unit Affirmation: I CAN ENJOY LIVING IN MY FAMILY!

 **Planning Ahead**

1. Photocopy Activity Sheets (pages 23 and 24)—one for each student.
2. Prepare six pieces of paper by writing one of the following family changes on each piece: Parent dies, Mom goes back to work full time, Parents divorce, A new baby, Family moves to a new state, A parent re-marries (step-family).

 Setting the Stage (5-10 minutes)
WHAT YOU'LL DO
- Play "Fruit Basket Upset" to introduce the idea of family changes

WHAT YOU'LL NEED
- The names of four fruits

 Introducing the Issue (20 minutes)
WHAT YOU'LL DO
- Prepare "Family Albums" to illustrate how various changes affect family life
- Use an activity sheet to see that change is a normal part of life
- Add a phrase to the Unit Affirmation poster

WHAT YOU'LL NEED
- Family changes pieces of paper
- "Nothing Stays the Same Forever" Activity Sheet (page 23)
- Unit Affirmation poster

 Searching the Scriptures (20 minutes)
WHAT YOU'LL DO
- Participate in a story to discover how God enabled a family to deal with changes

WHAT YOU'LL NEED
- Bibles
- Students' paper hearts from Families Lesson 1

 Living the Lesson (5-10 minutes)
WHAT YOU'LL DO
- Use an activity sheet to make finger puppets and role-play ways to handle family changes

WHAT YOU'LL NEED
- "Going Through the Changes" Activity Sheet (page 24)
- Scissors, tape

17

 # Lesson 2

Families

 ## Setting the Stage (5-10 minutes)

Before students arrive today, write the names of four fruits on the board, (such as apple, orange, banana, pear), and clear a space in your room large enough for everyone to sit on chairs in a circle. As kids enter the room, welcome them by whispering to each one the name of one of the fruits listed on the board, and ask them to be seated in the circle. As you whisper, repeat the names of fruit, so more than one child is assigned the same fruit. When several kids have arrived, start the game by designating one person as "IT". Ask "IT" to stand while you remove his or her chair from the circle. Be sure there is one less chair than the number of participants. "IT" starts the play by calling out the name of one of the fruits. Everyone who has been assigned that fruit must now stand up and move to a different chair, while "IT" also tries to find an empty chair. The person who does not get a chair is the new "IT" and calls out the next fruit. "IT" can also call out two of the fruits, or she or he may call out "FRUIT BASKET UPSET!", which signals everyone to get up and find a new seat. The game continues until time is called. **How did you feel when you had to change chairs? When you are playing "Fruit Basket Upset", making changes is fun. But sometimes changes happen in our families that can make life feel like everything is mixed up, much like "Fruit Basket Upset." It's usually not so fun to go through those changes. Today we will be talking about those times.**

 ## Introducing the Issue (20 minutes)

Have you ever wished that something in your life would never change or that a particular time would last forever? Let kids talk about this. Some examples might be: "I wished third grade would never end because I loved my teacher" "I wished my parents would never get a divorce" "I don't ever want to move away from our house." **There are many kinds of changes. Let's think of some. What is an example of a small change?** (Buy a new pair of shoes and throw the old ones away, rearrange the furniture in your bedroom.) **What is an example of a big change?** (A new teacher comes to your class mid-year, change schools.) **What is an example of a good change?** (The class bully moves away, relatives from out-of-town come to visit for two weeks.) **What is an example of a bad change?** (Best friend moves away, you start using drugs or alcohol.) **Did you know that human beings don't like change? Everyone feels a certain amount of discomfort when things change, even if it's a small change.** Illustrate this by asking your kids to put

Lesson 2

Families

their hands on the table and fold them, noticing which thumb is on top. Now have them unfold their hands and refold them, this time putting the other thumb on top. Ask them to describe how they feel when they do that. **That is just a little picture of how we react inside to changes in our lives. Now imagine how a big change can make you feel inside!**

Changes happen in families, too. Let's play a game to discover what some of those changes are. Divide your class into six groups (use fewer groups if you have less than 12 in your class) and give each group one of the pieces of paper with family changes written on them. Instruct the groups to prepare a "Family Album" that will tell the story of a family that is experiencing the change they have written on their slip of paper. They will have to work together to design a series of three or four pictures that will be drawn to look like snapshots. The first one should be of the family before the change takes place and the others of how the family was different because of the change. They cannot use words; their stories must be told through their family photo albums. When all the "albums" are complete, ask each group to show its pictures and let the rest of the class guess what the change is that happened in the family. When all the groups have made presentations, post the pictures around the room. Ask the class to think of any additional family changes that have not yet been mentioned. You might also ask kids who have experienced one or more of these changes in their families to share what it was like to go through that experience. NOTE: Remember that some changes are good changes, so be sure to include examples of these, too.

Distribute copies of the activity sheet, "Nothing Stays the Same Forever," (page 23). **Changes in our families can feel very upsetting and leave us feeling that something "bad" has happened or even that we are bad because of the change that has occurred. It can help to know that change is a normal, natural part of life. Everything changes, and as our poster says, "Nothing Stays the Same Forever." God tells us this in Ecclesiastes 3.** Look at the border of the poster and talk about all the different changes that are represented there. **What would happen if things never changed?** (The earth would be overrun with plants, animals and people if nothing ever died; we would be trapped in bad situations as well as good ones; we would never meet new friends.) Allow kids time to color their posters. As they work, remind them that when changes happen in their lives they can remember God's words in Ecclesiastes 3 and that nothing stays the same forever—ever!

Display the Unit Affirmation poster and read the Affirmation aloud together. **When changes happen in our families, especially big changes, it can feel like we will never enjoy living in them again. But we can get through**

Families

those changes by understanding that change is normal and we will eventually adjust to the change and move on with our lives. Write, "by accepting and adjusting to change when it comes" on the second line. We've already talked about accepting changes when they come; now let's see what we can discover about adjusting to changes by looking at what happened to one Bible family.

 Searching the Scriptures (20 minutes)

Close your eyes. Relax and listen as I tell you a story. When I ask a question don't answer it aloud, just think about your feelings. Imagine you are a part of the story.

Read or tell this story: You live in a foreign country because there is not enough to eat in your homeland. Your two older brothers marry women here. You all live together happily. Suddenly your father and brothers die. What are you feeling? Who will take care of you now? What will happen to all of you?

Your mother hears that God has now provided food in your homeland. She decides to go back. What are your thoughts? Your sisters-in-law start out with you, but your mom tells them to go home because she doesn't have any way to take care of them. How do you feel about this? The way to your homeland is dangerous and lonely. You and your mom need help. What will happen on the way?

One sister-in-law goes back. How do you feel now? The other sister-in-law refuses to leave. She begs to go with you. How do you feel about this? How do you think your mom feels?

Your mom tells her that if she comes with you, her life will be very hard. People won't treat her fairly. What do you think your sister-in-law is feeling? She wants to come anyway. She promises to stay with you and says only death can make her break her promise. How does this make you feel?

At last your mother agrees. The three of you go on together. How do you feel about this? What are you thinking? What will you do when you get to your new home?

Although you may have guessed, what I haven't yet told you is that your mother is Naomi and this sister-in-law is Ruth. Now open your eyes. Let's talk about this true story in the Bible. Have students turn to Ruth 1:1-18.

What changes had come to Naomi and Ruth's lives? (Naomi's husband and two sons had died; one of the sons had also been Ruth's husband.) This was a bad situation for these women. In biblical times widows were often very poor. People either took advantage of or ignored them. They

Families Lesson 2

had few rights. Many times they ended up as slaves or prostitutes. God saw to their care and protection by giving the people rules about widows marrying brothers or close relatives of husbands.

Check out verse 6. **What did Naomi hear about God after her family had died?** (He had given the Israelites food.) **What did she do when she heard this?** (Decided to go home.) **Naomi knew where to find help. She turned to God and God's people. The journey home would be hard and dangerous, yet she knew it was the right thing to do. Where do you seek help when changes come to your family?** Talk about available resources such as other family members, friends, church friends, counselors, psychologists, and social agencies as well as seeking God in prayer and reading His Word.

Look at verse 13. **How did Naomi grieve for the family members she had lost?** (Said the Lord's hand had gone out against her, was sad and bitter.) **Do you think it's wrong to grieve when you have lost someone or something dear to you?** Ask someone to read John 11:35, 36. **It's OK to grieve in situations like that. Even Jesus grieved when His good friend Lazarus died.**

Why do some people hesitate to be honest with others when they are sad or don't understand why God has allowed certain things to happen? Some people are afraid they won't be understood or others will think they really don't trust the Lord. **Some of the greatest people in the Bible questioned God about how or why things happened. God respects honest questions and loves to help us.**

How did Ruth react to Naomi's honesty? (She put Naomi's needs first and stayed to encourage her.) **When we share sorrows and questions with people who care about us, our relationships deepen. Then we can pray for and encourage each other.**

Check out verse 16. **What did Ruth say she wanted?** (To stay with Naomi and worship her God.) Ruth had seen Naomi turn to God in trouble as well as joy. Naomi believed the Lord was in control of everything and trusted Him to guide and care for her. Ruth wanted what Naomi had—a close relationship to God. Ruth and Naomi built their relationship around the Lord.

Do you think we should be honest about telling people what we want or need? Why or why not? Have someone read verses 17 and 18. **How did Ruth make her needs known to Naomi?** (Begged to go with her, promised that only death would separate her from Naomi.) **What was Naomi's reaction?** (She stopped arguing and allowed Ruth to come.)

This was not a case of merely begging for favors. The arrangement was of mutual benefit. Ruth faced racism and hard work to provide for Naomi. Later she included Naomi in the raising of her son, Obed. Naomi provided Ruth with

Lesson 2

Families

protection and encouragement in facing prejudice. She arranged a marriage for her even though it meant sharing her with someone else. Facing changes by working together for each other's benefit is a real advantage.

Ask students to read the Unit Verse, II Corinthians 6:18, together. **How does it make you feel when changes happen in your family?** (Scared, upset, unhappy.) **Would knowing this verse make a difference to you then? Why or why not?** Let students share their feelings. Focus on the loving care God wants to provide us. When we know that the all-powerful God wants to be our Father and will be with us, we can face changes without fear. Even if things are never the same again, we know that we can handle situations because God loves us and will help us work through them.

Distribute the paper hearts from Families, Lesson 1. Students will record ideas for their ideal families on them. **Remember that your "Ideal Family" is one that is exactly the way you would wish.** Next to the number two, have students write changes they can make to help mold their families more like their ideal.

 Living the Lesson (5-10 minutes)

Distribute copies of the activity sheet "Going Through the Changes" (page 24), scissors and tape. Briefly review the ways kids can handle changes in the family. These include: seeking God's help, grieving for what has been lost, saying what you need, and negotiating. Give the kids a few minutes to complete the speech balloons in each of the situations. Discuss what is taking place. **How do you think the characters are feeling? Why are they acting or reacting that way? What do you think makes us feel, act, or react that way? If they had to deal with another change like this what could they do differently?**

Praise God for His help in our times of family change. Pray that we will trust Him even when the future is unknown and allow Him to give us the help we need.

Nothing Stays the Same Forever!

Nothing Stays the Same Forever!

A time to be born...	...A time to die	A time to plant...	...A time to uproot	A time to be silent...
...A time to mend				...A time to speak
A time to tear...		**Nothing Stays the same forever!**		A time to weep...
...A time to give up				...A time to laugh
A time to search...		*Ecclesiastes 3: 1-8*		A time to mourn...
...A time to refrain	A time to embrace...	...A time to gather them	A time to scatter stones...	...A time to dance

Activity Sheet by Linda Kondracki © 1991 David C. Cook Publishing Co. Permission granted to reproduce for classroom use only.

Going Through the Changes

Bryan's mom and dad are divorced. He lives with his mom who now works full-time. She is very sad about the divorce. He only sees his dad one week-end a month. Bryan really misses his dad and would like to see more of him, but every time he comes, Mom gets upset.

Bryan is getting ready for his week-end with his dad. Mom has been watching him pack. What does Bryan say to his mom?

"I wish you wouldn't go today. The week-end is the only time I can spend time with you too, you know."

Kaci's Dad lost his job and hasn't been able to get another one. Money has been tight for the family. Mom and Dad seem to quarrel a lot lately. Kaci notices that her dad seldom talks to her and her little brother, Alex. Mom cries a lot and seems too busy to pay attention to them either. Kaci wants to talk to her parents about how neglected she and Alex feel.

One morning at breakfast Kaci says, "Mom and Dad . . .

Activity Sheet by Bev Gundersen © 1991 David C. Cook Publishing Co. Permission granted to reproduce for classroom use only.

Families

Lesson 3

I've Got a Secret

Aim: That your students will seek out God and also wise people who can help them when they suffer abuse in their families
Scripture: Matthew 18:1-7
Unit Verse: I will be a Father to you, and you will be my sons and daughters, says the Lord Almighty. II Corinthians 6:18
Unit Affirmation: I CAN ENJOY LIVING IN MY FAMILY

 Planning Ahead

1. Photocopy Activity Sheets (pages 31 and 32)—one for each student;
2. Due to the nature of this lesson, you may be told about serious abuse that is occurring in the family of one of your students. Many states have laws requiring this information be reported to authorities. Before this lesson, find out from your Senior Pastor your church's procedure for handling this kind of information.
3. Write the following three "secrets" on separate pieces of paper. "I have a boa constrictor for a pet." "I have 9500 baseball cards in my collection," and "We have 12 dogs and seven cats at our house."
4. Make and photocopy a list of resources as described in LIVING THE LESSON—one for each student.
5. Prepare "Road Signs to Help" poster as described in LIVING THE LESSON.

 Setting the Stage (5-10 minutes)
WHAT YOU'LL DO
- Play "I've Got a Secret" as an introduction to secrets

WHAT YOU'LL NEED
- Three "secrets" as described in PLANNING AHEAD, watch with a second hand

 Introducing the Issue (20 minutes)
WHAT YOU'LL DO
- Discuss abuses that occur in families and how they are usually kept as secrets
- Use an activity sheet to discover ways to tell secrets that should not be kept
- Add a phrase to the Unit Affirmation poster

WHAT YOU'LL NEED
- "To Tell or Not to Tell" Activity Sheet (page 32)
- Unit Affirmation poster

 Searching the Scriptures (20 minutes)
WHAT YOU'LL DO
- Use an activity sheet to notice God's warnings to those who abuse children and how God guides children

WHAT YOU'LL NEED
- Bibles
- "Why, God?" Activity Sheet (page 31)

 Living the Lesson (5-10 minutes)
WHAT YOU'LL DO
- Learn how to find resources to help protect kids from abuse

WHAT YOU'LL NEED
- Road Signs to Help" poster, resource list

25

Lesson 3

Families

> **SPECIAL NOTE FOR THIS LESSON:** As you teach this lesson, be aware that some of your students may be living in abusive situations of which you are totally unaware. Talking about secrets that are not OK to keep may give someone in your class the courage to tell you about his or her situation. You will need to prepare for this possibility in two ways: 1) Clearly tell your kids in advance that if they tell you about abuse in their families, you will do something to help change the situation. If you do not prepare them and then end up reporting something they tell you, they could view this as a serious breach of trust. 2) Know your church's procedure for handling this kind of situation. Your state laws most likely require you to report any evidence of actual abuse to authorities. If a child hints at abusive action, carefully and lovingly question that child in the presence of another trusted adult. Emphasize to the child that you will get help so the situation will end.

 ## Setting the Stage (5-10 minutes)

As your students arrive today, give three of them pieces of paper with "Secrets" written on them. Appoint a timekeeper to use a watch with a second hand. To begin the game, "I've Got a Secret," explain that the class is to find out each person's "secret" in two minutes by asking questions that can be answered only by yes or no. The first person with a "secret" starts by giving one very broad hint (such as, this is something I have at my house) before responding to questions. As time allows, other students may come up with ideas for unusual secrets and be questioned by the group.

How do you feel when you have a secret and everyone is trying to discover it? It can be fun when the secrets are made-up like those in our game. But secrets are true and they don't go away. We all have secret things in our lives no one knows. Some secrets our good to have and each of us has the right to keep some things private. Today we want to talk about another kind of secret. Some secrets can hurt us and those should not be kept private.

 ## Introducing the Issue (20 minutes)

Everyone has the right to keep some information about themselves secret. This is called privacy, and we all want our privacy respected. What are some examples of secrets we may choose to keep to ourselves?
Possibilities might include: liking a certain boy or girl, you might be moving but

26

Families

Lesson 3

you're not sure yet, your diary. **Part of the right to keep our secrets is the right to decide who we will tell our secrets to. It is an honor to be chosen as the one a friend will tell secrets to, and we must be careful to respect that honor by keeping their secrets a secret. Have you ever had a time when you chose to tell your secret to someone and that person did not keep your secret a secret?** Let kids share their experiences and feelings about telling and keeping secrets.

There are some secrets, however, that are *not OK* to keep secret. What are some examples of these kinds of secrets? A principle here is that any secret that covers up the fact that you or someone else is being hurt should *not* be kept secret. Examples include:

PHYSICAL ABUSE, when a child is being hit, punched, pushed, or hurt in other ways on an ongoing basis.

SEXUAL ABUSE, when a child is being touched in places and ways that are inappropriate and feel uncomfortable.

CHEMICAL ABUSE, when someone is using drugs or alcohol.

SUICIDE THREATS, when someone talks about killing himself or herself.

If you are suffering from one of these forms of abuse, *don't keep it a secret!* Tell someone you trust and get help! If you know of someone else in your family who is being abused or abusing themselves with drugs or thoughts of committing suicide, *don't keep it a secret*! It is *never OK* to let someone stay in a hurtful situation!

Distribute copies of the activity sheet, "To Tell or Not to Tell" (page 31). Ask kids to work together in pairs to fill in the first two questions in each story box. Talk about them together. **What will happen if Jason does not tell this secret?** (His brother will keep on using drugs and perhaps get into serious trouble.) **If he does tell?** (His brother may get mad at him, but at least he will get help.) **What will happen if Marissa does not tell her friend's secret?** (She will continue to be hurt by her father, perhaps seriously.) **What will happen if she does tell?** (Her friend may be very angry for breaking her trust, but at least she will get help and stop being hurt.) **What happened when Renae told her secret to her Mom?** (She didn't believe her.) **What might happen if she does not find someone else to tell?** (She will continue to be uncomfortable and perhaps hurt by her uncle.) **When we have secrets that should not be kept, it is important to know how to get help.** Divide the class into three groups and assign each group one of the stories. Ask them to fill in the last question and then plan a short skit depicting how their character can ask for help. Circulate among the groups as they work, making suggestions as needed. When they are finished, let each group present their skit to the rest of the class. **There are lots of ways to ask for help, and lots of people you can turn to when you need help. Who are some of them?** (Parents, teachers, neighbors, grandparents, pastors, Sunday school teachers,

Families

coaches, etc.) **If you are carrying a secret that needs to be told, you may be feeling scared that if you do tell someone, they won't believe or help you. Some adults may not. That's why it is important to have many names on your list of people who can help. If the first one does not help, try someone else. Keep talking to people until someone believes you and gets help!**

Display the Unit Affirmation poster and read the Affirmation aloud together. **It would be wonderful if all families were perfect families. But they aren't, and we need to do something when we or others in our families are being hurt.** Write, "by getting help when someone is being hurt" on the third line. **Now let's take a look at what Jesus says about kids who are hurting!**

Searching the Scriptures (20 minutes)

Have students take turns reading aloud Matthew 18:1-7. **What value did Jesus place on children?** (He called them the greatest in the kingdom of heaven.) **Why do you think He said that people had to change and needed to humble themselves like little children in order to enter the kingdom of heaven?** By nature, children trust others. They realize their helplessness and trust adults to provide for them. They believe that adults do things for their benefit. These natural characteristics help them to also trust God. Jesus wanted people to trust God as wholeheartedly as children did.

Jesus was very harsh about anyone who caused a child to sin. He warned that anyone who did this would receive a severe punishment. Why do you think He felt this way? If adults break their children's confidence in them, children no longer trust people. If they don't trust people, they can't really trust God either. This is a very serious matter to God.

Let's take a closer look at how God feels about abuse in our homes. Distribute copies of the activity sheet "Why, God?" (page 32). Choose two students to read the parts of the kid and God. Other students can follow along on their activity sheets.

In the drama why did God say He wouldn't just make parents stop abusing their children? (Because He gave them a free will; then they would only be puppets.) **God wants people to choose to love and follow Him. He won't interfere in our decisions, but lets us face the consequences. The Lord waits for us to ask Him for His help.**

The kid in the skit felt that it wasn't fair for children to have to suffer because of their parents' problems. What did the character "God" say about that? (God doesn't like it when kids suffer; life isn't always fair; problems don't all disappear quickly.)

In the play "God" said, "Just ask My servant Joseph about that." Have students

Families

Lesson 3

check out Genesis 37:28, 36; 39:20. **What kind of problems did Joseph have?** (His brothers sold him to slave traders, he became a slave in Egypt, he was falsely accused and put into prison.) Point out that even when Joseph did the right thing it led to more suffering. However, he never let his circumstances change who he was or his relationship with God. He trusted God and this allowed the Lord to work out His plan for Joseph's life. Ask someone to check out Genesis 45:5, 7. **How did Joseph feel about his problems later in life?** (They were all part of God's plan to save Joseph's family and others.)

The skit gave some ways that God guides abused kids. What were some of these methods? (Having them meet Christians; giving kids a desire for God; opportunity to accept Jesus and become members of God's family.) **What are some other ways God guides children?** Talk about giving us adults we can trust and who will help us such as family friends, pastors, Sunday school teachers, school counselors or nurses. Mature Christians who will be prayer partners without gossiping about problems can be very helpful to hurting kids. Sometimes foster homes can be places of protection for kids until home situations change and it is safe to return.

The drama gave some ways that kids can encourage their parents to see their need for God and His help. What were they? (Living the way God wants us to; praying for our parents; sharing Jesus with them in love.) **Things are not easy when there is abuse in our family, but when we follow Jesus and trust God to work things out in our lives there is hope for healing and forgiveness. God is the good Father and when you are on His team, you're a winner even when those around you do not believe in Jesus.**

Have students say II Corinthians 6:18 together. **Would knowing this verse be helpful to kids who are abused? Why or why not?** (Yes. It would be a comfort to know that God is a good Father who loves us and wants us as His children.) **You are of great value to God. You are His wonderful creation and He has a special plan for your life that will bring you good.** Help students understand that even though life is not always fair nor are all their problems solved quickly, God is always with them and does understand their problems.

Distribute the paper hearts from Families Lesson Two and continue the "Ideal Family List." Have kids write down any problems they would like to have removed from their families. Stress that this is a private matter and no one else will look at what they write. Many children will have no serious family problems and may need alternate suggestions such as "that we had more time to play together."

After #3 on the heart shape is completed, ask them to turn the hearts over. On the back side have them personalize the Unit Verse. For example: "I will be a Father to (Michael) and (Michael) will be my son, says the Lord Almighty." **Read this verse silently several times. Remember that this is God's desire and promise for you.**

 *Lesson 3* Families

Living the Lesson (5-10 minutes)

Before class, write the heading "Road Signs to Help" on a large sheet of poster board. List the hints shown, leaving a space in front of each tip for its sign.

 **Stop:** Don't argue when parents are angry

 **Caution:** Take care of yourself. Do what you need to do to make sure you are allright

 **U-turn:** Remove yourself. Go to your room or some other safe place

Yield: Tell God about it, ask for His protection and pray for the abuser

 **One-Way:** Talk about it. Tell a trusted adult

 **Detour:** Find an outside resource to help

There are a few practical tips kids can follow which may be of help. We will use road signs to help us see what they can do. As you offer the hints, draw the signs in the open spaces in front of them. Discuss the tips using questions like: **Why is this a good idea? What might happen if you do this? What might happen if you don't?**

Sometimes we need to look for outside resources to help us also. Distribute copies of the list you made before class. Discuss when it might be appropriate to contact someone for help. Include on your list outside resources that are available in your area for those who need help. Where possible, list names and telephone numbers. Some suggestions are: shelters, trained counselors, your state Department of Human Services, Sunday school teacher and pastor, a church home-shelter, Social Service Agencies, police, the National Child Abuse Hotline (1-800-422-4453). Free pamphlets which provide additional information on abuse can be obtained from the National Center for Missing and Exploited Children, 2101 Wilson Blvd., Ste. 550, Arlington, VA 22201.

Be sure everyone clearly understands what abuse is not (punishment because you have disobeyed, doing chores). Spend some time talking about how you and others you know receive Jesus' love through adults and family members. Encourage your students to do the same. Close with prayer, thanking God for all the kids in your class.

To Tell or Not to Tell...

Not all secrets should be kept. If you or someone you know is hurting themselves or being hurt by someone else, speak up! Tell a trusted adult and get help!

Jason knows his brother is using drugs.

What might happen if he does NOT tell this secret? _____
_____

What might happen if he does tell? _____
_____

What can Jason do to get help? _____
_____
_____

Marissa's best friend always has bruises and black eyes. Yesterday she came to school with a broken arm and told everyone she fell off her bike. But during recess, she whispered to Marissa that her Dad had pushed her down the stairs.

What might happen if Marissa does NOT tell her secret? _____
_____

What might happen if she does tell? _____
_____

What can Marissa do to get help? _____
_____

Renae's uncle is living with them for a few weeks. He likes to tuck her in bed and kiss her good night. Sometimes he touches her in ways that make her feel uncomfortable. She told her Mom, but she only said it was nothing. "He just loves you!"

What might happen if Renae does NOT tell someone else her secret? _____
_____

What might happen if she does tell? _____
_____

What can Renae do to get help? _____
_____

Activity Sheet by Linda Kondracki © 1991 David C. Cook Publishing Co. Permission granted to reproduce for classroom use only.

✓ Why, God?

KID: "Who is the greatest in the kingdom of heaven?"
GOD: "Whoever humbles himself like this child is the greatest in the kingdom of heaven."
KID: Is it really You, God? I was reading about Jesus and kids.
GOD: My Son and I love kids. "Whoever welcomes a little child . . . in my name welcomes me."
KID: If You love kids so much why do You let Dad hit me when he's been drinking? Why don't You help me?
GOD: I've been helping you a lot. I made it possible for you to meet people who know Me at Bible Club. I sent my Spirit to give you a desire for Me and an opportunity to become My child.
KID: I thought You would make my dad stop drinking and hitting me. Why didn't You do that?
GOD: It breaks My heart when your dad acts like that. But, I didn't make people to be like puppets. I gave them a free will. That means I only help people when they want Me to help. Your dad has a big problem. He needs to turn over his life to Me and ask Me to help him.
KID: I thought all my problems would disappear when I gave my life to You. Why haven't they? It isn't fair that I am the one who suffers. Kids shouldn't have to suffer because of parents.
GOD: You're right. I am unhappy when kids suffer. Life isn't always fair and problems don't always get solved quickly. Just ask My servant Joseph about that. However, you don't have to face things alone. I am here with you, I understand your problems, and I can help you take care of yourself.
KID: If I can't look to my parents to take care of me and my problems, who can I look to?
GOD: There are people around you who care about you and with whom you can talk. Look to your Sunday school teacher, teachers at school, school counselor, and the parents of some of your friends. And, I will help you. If you can learn to trust Me in your difficulties I can use even your problems for good.
KID: What good can come out of being abused?
GOD: You are very special to Me and I have a wonderful plan for your life. You only see a tiny bit of it now, like the pieces of a puzzle. Trust Me and I'll put the pieces together and work things out for you in the long run. If all the people in your family would see their needs and turn their lives over to Me, that's the best possible good.
KID: How can I help my parents see that they need You and Your help?
GOD: The same way you did. You learned about Me by seeing the way My followers lived. Their love, peace, and joy made you want what they had. Living My way, praying for your parents, and sharing Jesus with them in love will make them want to know Jesus, too.
KID: Thanks for answering some of my questions, God. It's not going to be easy though.
GOD: No, but remember, I'm with you. Together we're a winning team!

Activity Sheet by Bev Gundersen © 1991 David C. Cook Publishing Co. Permission granted to reproduce for classroom use only.

Families

Lesson 4

It Runs in the Family

Aim: That your students will commit themselves to caring for people in their families
Scripture: I Corinthians 13:4-7
Unit Verse: I will be a Father to you, and you will be my sons and daughters, says the Lord Almighty. II Corinthians 6:18
Unit Affirmation: I CAN ENJOY LIVING IN MY FAMILY!

 **Planning Ahead**

1. Photocopy Activity Sheets (pages 39 and 40)—one for each student.
2. Prepare 28 letter cards (approximately 6"x 6" each) to spell out the phrase: "Love each other as I have loved you." Write only one letter on each card.
3. Prepare a mural background by cutting a four-foot length of butcher or shelf paper and writing "A Garden of Family Caring" as a heading across the top. Add grass along the bottom and a sun in one corner.
4. Cover table tops with newsprint or butcher paper for "Doodling Discussion."
5. Prepare balloons for "Love Balloons" game as described in LIVING THE LESSON.

 Setting the Stage (5-10 minutes)
WHAT YOU'LL DO
- Play a game to introduce the idea of loving one another in our families

WHAT YOU'LL NEED
- Letter cards

 Introducing the Issue (20 minutes)
WHAT YOU'LL DO
- Make a mural to identify ways family members care for one another
- Use an activity sheet to make affirmation cards as one way to care for others in our families
- Add a phrase to the Unit Affirmation poster

WHAT YOU'LL NEED
- Mural background
- "Care Cards" Activity Sheet (page 39)
- Unit Affirmation poster

 Searching the Scriptures (20 minutes)
WHAT YOU'LL DO
- Use an activity sheet to complete a crossword puzzle to discover how God wants families to love one another

WHAT YOU'LL NEED
- Bibles
- "Love in Action" Activity Sheet (page 40)

 Living the Lesson (5-10 minutes)
WHAT YOU'LL DO
- Express ways to care for family members by pantomiming action words

WHAT YOU'LL NEED
- "Love Balloons", opened-up paper clip

 Families

✓ Setting the Stage (5-10 minutes)

Before class, pin the 28 letter cards to a bulletin board or attach them to the wall in the correct order of the phrase, but with the letters facing the wall so they cannot be seen. To play this game, let kids take turns guessing a letter of the alphabet. If the letter is on one of the cards, turn the card(s) over so it can be read. Continue letting students take turns guessing letters until someone guesses the phrase correctly. **Who recognizes this phrase?** (It is Jesus' words to His disciples, found in John 15:12.) **Jesus said these words to His disciples because He knew that loving each other is hard work, and they would have to learn how to do it. The same is true in our families. Today we want to talk about ways we can learn to love and care for each other as a way to make our families good places for everyone who lives in them.**

✓ Introducing the Issue (20 minutes)

Before class, attach the mural background to the wall where kids will have easy access to work on it. **We tend to think of families as places where everyone automatically loves and cares for each other. But that is not necessarily true! It takes time, effort, and work to learn how to care for one another in our families. It can help to think about it like growing a garden. To think that families automatically love and care for each other is like saying all you have to do to grow a garden is plant seeds. What do we need to know if we want to grow a healthy garden?** Write the word "KNOWLEDGE" on the board. **What else do we need to know to grow a garden?** (Where to place it so the plants will get the right amount of sun, how and when to fertilize, the difference between young plants and weeds, how much to water.) Write the word "TIME" on the board. **How much time does it take to grow a garden?** (Lots of time to care for the garden's needs. You have to set aside regular amounts of time to keep up with it as it grows.) Write the word "EFFORT" on the board. **How much effort does it take to grow a garden?** (Gardening is hard work. It takes commitment to do all the work of planting, weeding, fertilizing, watering.)

Learning to care for each other in our families takes the same things as growing a garden. Point to the word "KNOWLEDGE" on the board. **What do we need to know to care for other family members?** (What makes them happy, sad, mad, what they like and don't like, what irritates them, what should be respected as private, etc.) Point to the word "TIME" on the board.

Lesson 4

Families

How much time does it take to care for other family members? (Being with each other, listening to each other, and doing acts of kindness for each other all takes lots of time!) Point to the word "EFFORT" on the board. **How much effort does it take to care for other family members?** It's hard work to care for other's needs. Sometimes we may not feel like doing acts of kindness or listening or being with others in our families. During those times, we can make the effort to do what is needed.

Distribute colored paper and scissors and instruct the kids to cut out flowers to add to the mural background. On each flower, they can write something that would be an example of caring for others in their families. Have the kids discuss what they will write on their flowers, so they all will write something different. Possibilities might include: Cleaning my room without being told, playing with my brother so Mom can rest, writing notes to family members, staying out of other's rooms and things, giving hugs, praying for family members. The list is endless! Help your kids come up with creative ideas. When the flowers are finished, kids can add them to the mural.

> **OPTIONAL:** If you have time, kids who finish early could be instructed to draw weeds and insects for the garden, writing on these pieces things that hurt or destroy family caring. Possibilities might include: fighting, reading someone's diary, always complaining about chores, name-calling.

Distribute copies of the activity sheet "Care Cards" (page 39). **One way we can care for others in our families is by sending notes. As you work on these little cards, be thinking about which ones you would like to give to each member of your family.**

Write something you know he or she would like to hear. Allow time for completion of the cards.

Display the Unit Affirmation poster and read the Affirmation aloud together. **What phrase could we add to the next line?** Let kids give suggestions. Choose one that says something like "by taking time to care for others!" and

 *Lesson 4*   Families

write it on the fourth line. **Loving and caring for family members is not always easy. Now let's look at a very important chapter in the Bible to discover what God says about loving others.**

 Searching the Scriptures (20 minutes)

Today you will be studying I Corinthians 13:4-7, the famous love passage. Because kids are bombarded by the media with so many false ideas about love, your Juniors get the impression that it is only a sort of "gooey feeling" people have towards the opposite sex. Love is confused with lust. Lust is selfish. It is wanting someone who gives us pleasure. Love is not a feeling, but an action. It's something we decide to do to express our caring concern for others.

Have someone look up and read aloud I John 4:8b. **How does this verse describe love?** (God is love.) **In the next verse** (I John 4:9) **we find how God showed us His love. What did He do?** (Sent His Son, Jesus, to provide salvation for us.) Point out that God did something to show us He was love. Ask someone to read verse 11. **What does this verse tell us we should do about love?** (Love one another.) **Why should we do this?** (Because God loves us.) **True love is directed towards others. It is seen when a person unselfishly cares for and serves others.**

Do you think it is easy or difficult to show love to family members? Let kids respond. **Why do you think it is often harder to show love to family members than to other people?** When we are with outsiders we often put on an act to appear other than we are. Our families knows what we are really like. They see us when we are at our worst as well as when we are at our best. This knowledge sometimes makes it difficult to love our family. It is also the reason we need to make special efforts to demonstrate God's love, and our love to each other.

Why do you think we should express our love to our families? Family members often take each other for granted. While it is our parents' role to provide food and clothing for us, point out that they show their love to us by giving us our favorite foods and clothes in the colors and styles we want. When families express their care for each other everyone is encouraged and built up in love.

Have students turn to I Corinthians 13:4-7 in their Bibles. Distribute copies of the activity sheet "Love in Action" (page 40). Read the directions and let students work on this individually or in pairs. Completing this crossword puzzle is fun and also provides an in-depth study of what real love is and how

Families

Lesson 4

it works. Across answers are: 1-patient, 3-hope, 6-perseveres, 8-angered, 10-trust, 11-protect, 12-self-seeking, 14-envy. Down answers are: 1-proud, 2-kind, 4-truth, 7-rude, 9-boast, 13-envy. After they have completed this activity, go over the puzzle words and their definitions to make sure that kids clearly understand what is meant.

Paul gives us two lists in this Scripture passage. Let's look at them. Write these lists on the board or a large sheet of poster board so everyone can see them. Make two columns entitled "Love Is " and "Love Is Not." "Love Is" items are: patient, kind, glad with the truth, protecting of others, trustful, hopeful, always persevering. "Love Is Not" items are: envious, boastful, proud, self-seeking (selfish), angry, a record-keeper of wrongs, delightful in evil. **If we look closely at these lists we can see that the positive "Love Is" things all affect how we treat others. The negative "Love Is Not" things all center on ourselves. To sum it up, what Paul is saying in these verses is that love is an action we do for others.**

Keep your lesson upbeat by discussing the positive ways we can care for people in our families. Put a pile of crayons or markers in the center of the table(s) covered with paper. Conduct the "Doodle Discussion" by letting students doodle while you talk about these things together. Invite them to talk about their doodles at the end of the discussion.

Discuss the words you listed in the "Love Is" column. For example, when using the word "patience", focus on questions similar to these: **When do family members need to be patient with each other? Do you need to be more patient with some members of your family than others? Who? Why? What can you do to show your love for that person?** Encourage your kids to be as specific as possible about ways to show love for family members in each case.

Because each family is unique, different family members may be highlighted for different words. Some examples are: parents protect their children. This shows their care for them. Children show love for their parents by trusting them and the plans and decisions they make for the family.

Have students turn to II Corinthians 6:18 and say it together. **What are some ways that God takes care of us every day?** (He gives us food, air to breathe, clothing, shelter, families, friends, joy, protection from harm.) **God shows His care for us in all these ways. He treats us like His children by providing for all our needs. The Unit Verse is a promise from God that we can trust will happen to us. Our heavenly Father delights in showing us His love when we trust in Him.**

Distribute the "Ideal Family" paper hearts from Families Lesson Three. Today students will write gifts they would like to give their families by number four.

Lesson 4

Families

Have them include in these gifts some non-material ones such as peace, perfect health, joy, and knowing Jesus as their Savior.

☑ Living the Lesson (5-10 minutes)

Before class, prepare balloons for a team charades game. Write four to six ways to express love to families on pieces of paper. Some examples are: share a smile, help with dishes, be a good listener, tell a family member you love him or her, give a hug, share a treat, compliment your sister or brother, write a "love you" note, run an errand for a busy parent, brag about your sister or brother to your parent(s). Place a piece of paper inside each balloon, then blow up the balloon and tie it.

Clear a playing space in your room. Divide your class into two teams. A player from one team pops a balloon with the open end of a paper clip, shows the paper to team members and they act it out. The other team has one minute to guess what the action represents. Then the other team pops a balloon and acts out the activity on its paper. Depending on time, give each team two or three turns.

Regather the group. **We've talked about how to care for our families and acted out ways to do it. Think about the things we studied today and choose one of them to do for your family this week.** Close by having students pray silently, asking God to help them show their family they love them.

Care Cards ✓

Make a Care Card to give to each member of your family. Write your own slogan on the cards that are blank. Say something special that you know your family will enjoy! Leave these cards on pillows, in lunch boxes, on the bathroom mirror, taped to the milk carton and other places they will enjoy finding them!

You're fun to be with!	You're growing up Great!
#1 _____	I ♥ U!
I'll pray for you today!	YOU'RE MY FAVORITE SISTER-

Activity Sheet by Linda Kondracki © 1991 David C. Cook Publishing Co. Permission granted to reproduce for classroom use only.

Love in Action

Real love is an action. Look in I Corinthians 13:4-7 to see what it is and how it works. Read the clues and complete the puzzle to find out more about the kind of love we can express to our families.

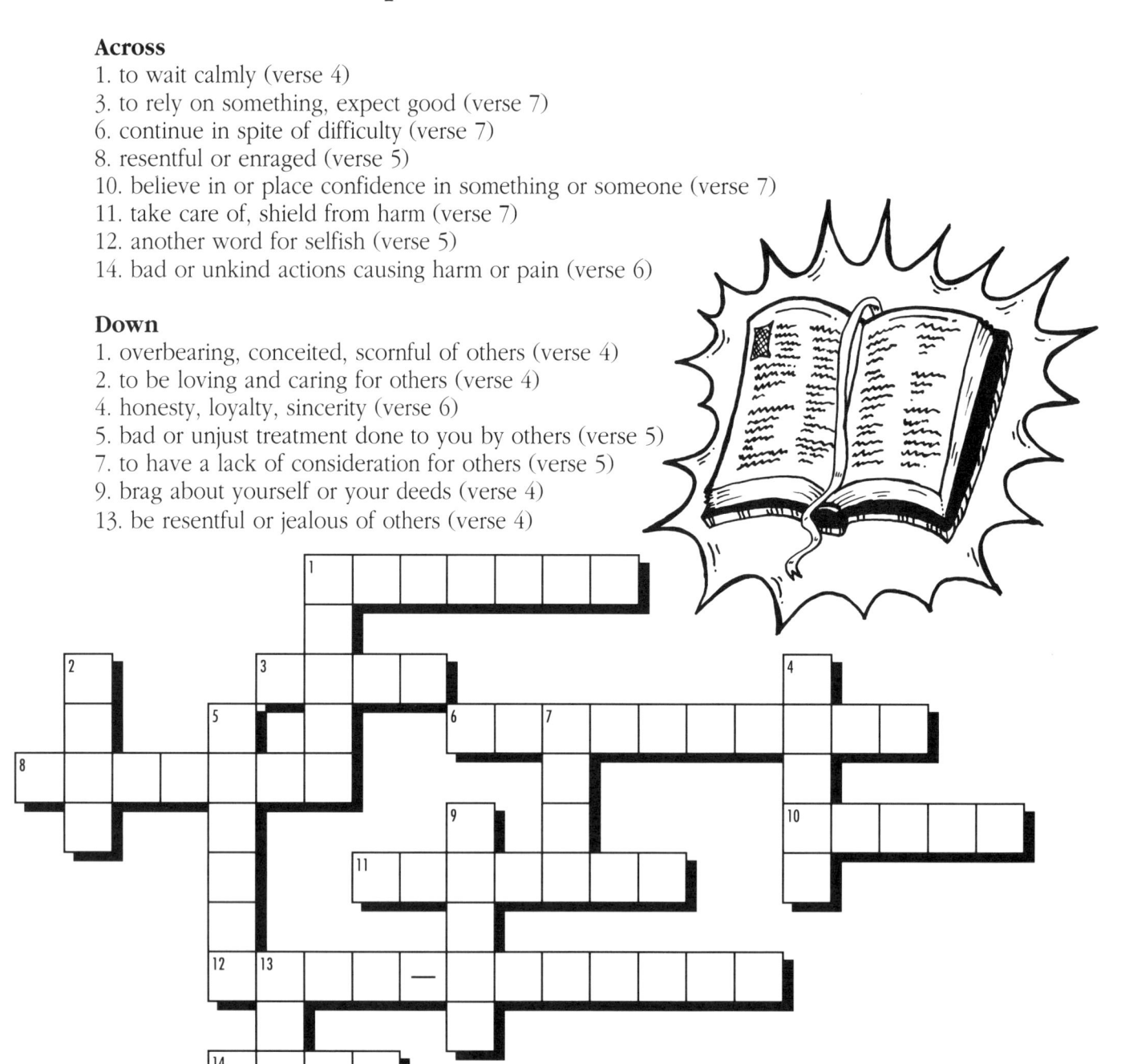

Across
1. to wait calmly (verse 4)
3. to rely on something, expect good (verse 7)
6. continue in spite of difficulty (verse 7)
8. resentful or enraged (verse 5)
10. believe in or place confidence in something or someone (verse 7)
11. take care of, shield from harm (verse 7)
12. another word for selfish (verse 5)
14. bad or unkind actions causing harm or pain (verse 6)

Down
1. overbearing, conceited, scornful of others (verse 4)
2. to be loving and caring for others (verse 4)
4. honesty, loyalty, sincerity (verse 6)
5. bad or unjust treatment done to you by others (verse 5)
7. to have a lack of consideration for others (verse 5)
9. brag about yourself or your deeds (verse 4)
13. be resentful or jealous of others (verse 4)

Activity Sheet by Bev Gundersen © 1991 David C. Cook Publishing Co. Permission granted to reproduce for classroom use only.

Families

Lesson 5 ✓

Part of the Family of God

Aim: That your students will choose to follow Jesus and become part of God's family
Scripture: Galatians 4:4-7
Unit Verse: I will be a Father to you, and you will be my sons and daughters, says the Lord Almighty. II Corinthians 6:18
Unit Affirmation: I CAN ENJOY LIVING IN MY FAMILY!

✓ Planning Ahead

1. Photocopy Activity Sheets (pages 47 and 48)—one for each student.
2. Find someone to do the skit as described in INTRODUCING THE ISSUE. OPTIONAL: If you have a VCR available for your class, record two or three minutes of a family sitcom that portrays the "perfect" family, such as the Cosby Show. Select a segment that shows a particularly "perfect" scene, such as the family happily all talking together, or the father solving a problem with great wisdom. Have the tape ready to play as the skit begins.
3. Prepare "Mission Impossible" as described in SEARCHING THE SCRIPTURES.

1. Setting the Stage (5-10 minutes)
WHAT YOU'LL DO
- Play a circle game about our families

WHAT YOU'LL NEED
- Chairs set in a circle

2. Introducing the Issue (20 minutes)
WHAT YOU'LL DO
- Present a skit to illustrate the fact that there are no perfect families, and talk about the imperfections in our own families
- Use a worksheet to identify the benefits of belonging to God's family
- Complete the Unit Affirmation poster

WHAT YOU'LL NEED
- "God Invites ME to Join His Family!" Activity Sheet (page 47)
- Unit Affirmation poster

3. Searching the Scriptures (20 minutes)
WHAT YOU'LL DO
- Discover God's desire and provision for every person to become His child by becoming "Mission Impossible" detectives

WHAT YOU'LL NEED
- Bibles
- "Mission Impossible" materials

4. Living the Lesson (5-10 minutes)
WHAT YOU'LL DO
- Use an activity sheet to write a letter to God considering the opportunity to become a member of His family

WHAT YOU'LL NEED
- "A Letter Home" Activity Sheet (page 48)

Lesson 5

Families

✓ Setting the Stage (5-10 minutes)

As your students arrive today, ask them to take a chair and sit in a circle. There must be only as many chairs in the circle as there are kids. When new kids arrive, they can join the circle by adding a chair to it. Begin this Circle Game* by telling the class that you will be reading a number of statements about their families. They are to listen carefully to each one, and if it is true about their family, they must follow the directions you will give. If it is not true, they must remain seated in their chairs. They must follow the directions precisely, even if it means sitting in a chair where someone else is already seated. (In some cases, kids may end up sitting on each other's laps three or four deep!)

1. If you have a mother and father living in your house, move two chairs to the right.
2. If you have a younger brother, move three chairs to the right.
3. If you have two grandfathers who are still alive, move one chair to the left.
4. If you have two sisters, move two chairs to the left.
5. If you have only one parent living in your house, move four chairs to the left.
6. If you have a stepparent, move two chairs to the right.
7. If you have a dog at your house, move one chair to the right.
8. If you wish you had a dog at your house, move two chairs to the right.
9. If you have a grandparent who lives in a state other than the one you live in, move three chairs to the left.
10. If you ate Christmas dinner with some of your cousins, move one chair to the left.

As you can see, all our families are different. But they all have one thing in common. None of our families is perfect! Today we will talk about what that means.

✓ Introducing the Issue (20 minutes)

Before class, prepare the following skit. For the "perfect" family segment, either pantomime a "perfect" family scene using several students as family members or use a VCR as described in PLANNING AHEAD.

WHAT'S WRONG WITH MY FAMILY?*
CHARACTERS: Joey, Mother.

Families

Lesson 5

JOEY enters and turns on TV. He watches some of the segment of a "Perfect Family" without saying anything.

MOTHER: (Enters and shuts off TV.) How many times have I told you, no TV until your room is clean and your homework done. You got a D on your last geography test. Have you done your geography homework yet?
JOEY: Not yet, but I'll do it right after this show is over!
MOTHER: I said NO. Now go to your room. And when your father comes home, he'll have something to say to you! (Exits.)
JOEY: (Pouting) HUMPH! My father. He never comes home! Last week he missed my Little League game 'cause he had to work. He's always working. (Thinks for a moment) I'll bet Dr. Huxtable never misses any of his kids' games. I hate my family! We're always yelling at each other. Oh well. (Pause) I think I'll call Billy. Maybe his family would let me come and live with them. His family is really neat. Except for his sister. She's always calling him names. But even so, living in his family would be better than living in mine! (Pretends to dial phone.)

Have you ever wished you lived in a different family? Allow for responses. **It's normal for us to look around and compare what it's like living in our family to what we think it would be like to live in other families. What do you think Billy will say when Joey tells him he'd rather live in Billy's family?** (He'll probably laugh and say he's not so crazy about living in his family, either! Don't forget about his little sister.) **Because our families are not perfect, it is easy for us to look around and wish we could find a different one. Sometimes when our families do not, or cannot meet our needs, we may even make up an imaginary family in our minds and pretend we belong to it. But neither of those options will help us get through the times when our families are not meeting our needs.**

Explain to your class that there is another family we can belong to that will help us in ways our own cannot. There is a family with a loving Father who wants to adopt us and take care of us. This family also has lots of people in it who care for one another in special ways. That Father is God, and His family is the church. **We can belong to God's family at the same time we belong to our own family. In fact, we very much need both families!**

Distribute copies of the activity sheet, "God Invites ME to Join His Family!" (page 47). Work together to fill in the blanks on the top half. The answers are: Because He loves you; By believing in Jesus, Eternally. Then have the students look at the pictures and write statements about the benefits of living in God's

Lesson 5

Families

family as illustrated by the pictures. Suggested statements are: God is always with us, God's Word teaches us how to live, and The Church Family is my family too!

Display the Unit Affirmation poster and read the affirmation aloud together. Then add a phrase to complete it. Possibilities might include: by belonging to God's family, too; or, by accepting that it's not perfect. **It would be nice if we all lived in perfect families. But even if we did, we would want to belong to God's family, too. Now let's look at what the Bible says about how we become a member of God's family.**

✓ Searching the Scriptures (20 minutes)

Before class, prepare for the "Mission Impossible" activity. You will need the following materials: cassette-player, blank cassette, picture of Adam and Eve, 9" x 12" manila envelope, three sheets of 8 1/2" x 11" paper; four 3" x 5" cards.

Enlist the help of a friend to tape the following message for you on a cassette. The • indicates a slight pause in the tape.

"Good day, Dr. Helps. Sin entered the world through the disobedience of this pair, Adam & Eve.• As a result, God's enemy • held as hostages the people God created to be His children. When the right time came God sent a secret agent to earth on a mysterious assignment. Your mission, should you accept it, is to find out the identity of this secret agent, the assignment He was given, and the results of His work.• Start by following the clues in Galatians 4:4-7.• Should you or any of your team decide to accept His provision, the Lord will acknowledge you as part of His family. This tape will self-destruct in thirty seconds."

Be prepared to play the cassette on a tape-player. Put a picture of Adam and Eve in a manila envelope along with three sheets of paper on which you have printed in large print these signs: God's enemy SATAN, ?, Read Galatians 4:4-7 aloud. Also prepare question-clue cards on four index cards.

1. What hostages are involved? Galatians 4:5; Isaiah 53:6; Romans 3:23
2. Who is the secret agent? Galatians 4:4; Matthew 1:21; Acts 4:10-12
3. What was the purpose of the secret mission? Galatians 4:5; John 3:16, 17; Ephesians 1:4, 5
4. What were the results of this secret mission? Galatians 4:5-7; Romans 8:15-17

Place these cards and four pencils in different corners of the room before students arrive.

This tape and envelope were delivered here by a secret messenger. He asked that we listen to the tape and open the envelope now. Play the cassette and pull out the pictures of Adam and Eve and the signs when mentioned on the taped message (as indicated by the • in the written text above). Invite the kids to join with you in this adventure and follow the clues to solve

Families

Lesson 5

the mystery.

Have students complete the first clue together and take turns reading Galatians 4:4-7 aloud. Divide the group into four teams. Send one team to each corner of the room to check out a question and clues. Allow a few minutes for them to find and write down the answers on the cards. Regroup, discuss their findings, and write them on the board. Be sure to praise each team for uncovering the evidence from their clues.

Who were the hostages? (Those under the law.) Explain that this phrase means everyone who fails to keep all of God's commandments. **What did your clues say about keeping God's laws?** (All people have broken God's laws and gone their own way, all people are sinners.) Point out that each of us is guilty. Adam and Eve were the first sinners, but because we are human and like to run our lives ourselves, we are just as guilty as they were.

Who is the secret agent? (Jesus, God's Son.) **What did you discover about His name?** (He was named Jesus, meaning "Savior" because He would save people from their sins.) **What unique job does He have?** (He is the only one who can save people from sin.)

What was the purpose of His mission? (To save the world, all people, from sin; adopt us as God's children; give us full rights.) **When was this mission planned?** (Before the creation of the world.) Point out that this was not a "last-minute" decision, but God's purpose for us even before people were created or sin separated us from our heavenly Father.

What were the results of His mission? (We can be saved from being slaves to sin, made heirs with Jesus, part of God's family, can receive the Holy Spirit who allows us to call God our Father.) Unfortunately the name "father" carries a bad association for some children today. In cases where fathers have abused or molested their children, the idea of calling God their father is not a pleasant thought. Be aware of kids who have had this experience. Help them to think of God as much more than even the "perfect" human father could be—the ideal father who cares for their welfare more than his own selfish purposes. The word "Abba" is an endearing term meaning "dearest daddy" and carries with it great warmth and love.

Under the law adopted children receive all the same benefits of biological children. They share equally in all the property of their fathers. This means that when we become adopted children of God we share equally with Jesus in all of God's resources.

Ask students to say II Corinthians 6:18 together. **Although there are no perfect families here on earth we can become a part of God's family and have Jesus Christ as our older brother.**

Distribute the paper hearts from Families Lesson Four. Have students complete their pattern for ideal families by writing dreams or goals they have for

✓ Lesson 5

Families

them. Kids can take these hearts home and use them as reminders that they can help make their families more like their ideal by doing every day the things they learned in this unit.

✓ Living the Lesson (5-10 minutes)

God's desire for us is to become members of His family. Jesus made it possible for people to reach that goal and become God's children by His sinless life and willing death. Jesus turned the mission impossible into mission possible. How can we enjoy the benefits He gained for all people? Have someone read aloud John 1:12, 13. Make the way of salvation plain to your students. **We have to trust that Jesus is the Savior God sent to save us and that He has paid the price for our sin. Then we accept Him as our personal Savior by asking Him to forgive our sins. We turn our lives over to Him to guide and control.**

Distribute copies of the activity sheet "A Letter Home" (page 49). **Think about the verse at the top of this page. Then write a letter to God by completing the sentences.** Some of your students may have already received Jesus as their Savior and might want to express praise or thanksgiving in their letters. Others may be considering making a decision to receive Jesus. Still others may have questions or may not be at all interested. Each student will be at a different place in their spiritual development. Encourage your students to write a letter to God expressing what they think about John 1:12 or how they would like to respond to the verse. **If you want to become a member of God's family, write that. If you have some questions or uncertainties about being in God's family, you can write about those. If you have already accepted God's provision for you to become His child, write an affirmation of that decision and how you would like to improve your relationship with your heavenly Father.**

Explain that by dating their decision students can look back on this day as their spiritual birthday. In the future, if they are troubled by doubts about whether they are part of God's family, they can refer to this date and know that it was the day they chose to receive Jesus as God's provision for them to become a child of God.

Encourage the kids who chose to accept Jesus as their Savior to tell you or a friend about it. Close in prayer, thanking God for His desire and provision for us to become members of His forever family.

* © 1990 Confident Kids Support Groups: Program Guide, Unit II Used by permission.

God Invites ME to Join His Family! ✓

The missing words below are in John 3:16. Can you find them and complete the answers to the questions?

Why? Because He _____ you.
How? By _____ in Jesus.
For How long? _____.

John 3:16
For God so loved the world that he gave his one and only Son, that whoever believes in him shall not perish, but have eternal life.

Living in God's Family Means...

(Panel 1: A boy praying — "DEAR GOD, THANK YOU FOR HELPING ME IN SCHOOL TODAY...")

(Panel 2: A child reading the Bible)

(Panel 3: A girl walking to church)

Activity Sheet by Linda Kondracki © 1990 Confident Kids Support Groups: Program Guide. Used by permission.
Permission granted to reproduce for classroom use only.

✓ A Letter Home

"Yet to all who received him, to those who believed in his name, he gave the right to become children of God." John 1:12

(date)_____

Dear God,
I thank You for _____
_____
_____
_____.

I want to _____
_____
_____.

Please _____
_____
_____
_____.

(signed)

Activity Sheet by Bev Gundersen © 1991 David C. Cook Publishing Co. Permission granted to reproduce for classroom use only.

Junior Electives

Service Projects For Families

In addition to the projects listed in these lessons, your class or church can also serve in the following ways:

✓ 1. Invite someone who has recovered from a hurting experience to share with you and your group. Discuss God's love and healing for the times we are hurt even if we are innocent.

✓ 2. Stage a "Family Appreciation" party and invite families for an evening of fun, food, and fellowship. Serve a simple meal kids can help fix and let them plan some games or songs that include all ages. Include a sharing time when family members can talk about good memories together.

✓ 3. Start an "adopt a grandparent" program pairing your students with elderly people in your church or a nursing home. Many families today don't have the joy of including extended members such as grandparents.

✓ 4. Work together on how to plan a family event such as a meal, camp-out, or hike. Make sure the plan includes each family member by having jobs appropriate for every age, physical ability, and talent.

✓ 5. Sponsor a "Family Parade" where entire families participate as units. Choose a theme such as "Gifts from God." Make it a non-motorized parade where baby strollers, wagons, trikes, bikes, even wheelchairs can be decorated with streamers, balloons, and signs.

Junior Electives

The Environment

Join the "E" Team!

What's the "E" Team? It's everyone working together to wipe out "Earth Abuse!" During this unit on environmental concerns, your students will be challenged to become "E" Team members as they look for ways they can help care for our beautiful world.

With all the concern for the environment in our society these days, this will probably not be the first time your Juniors will have discussed this issue. In fact, some of your students may be feeling quite anxious about all they have heard. It can be scary to be told that your planet is in danger of running out of resources or being destroyed by harmful rays from the sun! Being children, they can easily feel the problem is big and overwhelming and, in comparison, they are small and helpless. In the weeks ahead, you will be able to reassure them that the only real solution to this big problem is for everyone to do small things to help. When we multiply the small things that even kids can do easily with the number of people doing them, the problem is easily solved!

During this unit, you will also take your students to Scripture to see the wonderful gift our planet is to us, and that caring for it properly is a part of what God intended when He gave it to us. By the end of the unit, they will see our world not just as a planet in trouble, but as a beautiful place to live and enjoy!

The Environment Overview

Unit Verse: It is required that those who have been given a trust must prove faithful.
I Corinthians 4:2.

Unit Affirmation: I CAN ENJOY LIVING IN MY WORLD!

LESSON	TITLE	OBJECTIVE	SCRIPTURE BASE
Lesson #1	Our Unique Planet	That your students will thank God for creating, maintaining, and giving the earth to us.	Psalm 104:1-31
Lesson #2	A World Full of Wonder	That your students will develop an appreciation for the diversity found in God's creation.	Genesis 1:1-27; Selected Scriptures
Lesson #3	Caretakers of Earth	That your students will know that God appointed people to become caretakers of the earth and we are accountable to God for protecting it.	Genesis 2:2-9, 15, 18-23; Leviticus 25:1-7, 18-22
Lesson #4	United, We Save	That your students will determine to do something as a group to praise God for our Earth by helping to save and protect it.	Psalm 148:1-13

Partners ✓

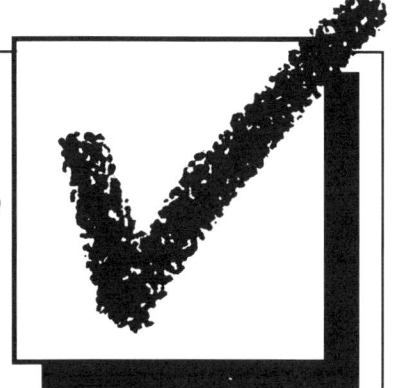

Keeping Parents Informed and Involved!

For the next few weeks your Junior-age child will be part of a group learning about The Environment. *Partners* is a planned parent piece to keep you informed of what will be taught during this exciting series.

PREVIEW...

The Environment

Kids today are being told a lot about the need to take better care of our planet. So much so, that many are feeling quite anxious about all they are hearing. It can be frightening to think that there might not be a planet when they grow up, and they can easily feel small and paralyzed in the face of such a big and overwhelming problem! In the next few weeks your children will see that caring for our planet need not be as overwhelming as it may sound. The fact of the matter is, the only real solution to this big problem is for everyone to do small things to help: things that even kids will find easy and fun to do. When we multiply these small things with the number of people doing them, the problem is easily solved!

During this unit, your children will also learn from Scripture what a wonderful gift our planet is to us, and that caring for it properly is a part of what God intended when He gave it to us. As they review the Unit Verse and Unit Affirmation each week, they will be encouraged to see our world not just as a planet in trouble, but as a beautiful place to live and enjoy!

Unit Verse:

It is required that those who have been given a trust must prove faithful. I Corinthians 4:2

Unit Affirmation:

I CAN ENJOY LIVING IN MY WORLD!

PRINCIPLES...

The Environment

PRINCIPLE #1:

OUR WORLD IS A GIFT FROM GOD. Before God created human beings, He prepared a beautiful and perfect environment for them. In a way, it was like a loving parent preparing a nursery for an expected new baby. With care, a parent provides everything the child will need to be comfortable and healthy. That's a description of God's creative work in Genesis 1. Although it isn't quite the paradise it was when God first created it, it is important for our kids to see that our world is still a beautiful and wonderful place to live!

PRINCIPLE #2:

CARING FOR OUR WORLD IS A RESPONSIBILITY FROM GOD. Along with describing the loving way God created our world, Genesis 1 and 2 also tell us of the responsibility He gave to humans to take care of it. For Christians, taking environmental concerns seriously is not only necessary to insure the survival of our planet, it is also a God-given responsibility.

PRINCIPLE #3:

EARTH ABUSE IS EVERYONE'S PROBLEM. In the weeks ahead, your kids will learn that when we treat the earth as if it will last forever, or tell ourselves that "this one little thing won't matter," we are committing "Earth Abuse." The six forms of Earth Abuse they will discuss are:

©1991 David C. Cook Publishing Co. Permission granted to reproduce for distribution to parents only.

Partners

#1: Air pollution
Harmful gases from factories and cars keep pouring into the air, making it unsafe for people and animals to breathe.

#2: Ozone layer
Gases used in the cooling units of air conditioners and refrigerators, plastic foam, and some aerosol cans are damaging the layer of ozone that protects us from harmful rays from the sun. If this continues, people on earth will die from over exposure to the sun.

#3: Wasting water
The earth has the same amount of water no matter how many people live on it. With more people on earth than ever before, we have to use less to be sure there is enough for everyone.

#4: Wasting energy
Factories that burn coal and oil to generate electricity pollute the air; the less energy we use, the less they have to run.

#5: Too much garbage
When garbage is thrown away, it is taken to landfills and buried where it decomposes and becomes part of the earth again. However, so much of our garbage today is made of materials that don't decompose, and our landfills are overflowing!

#6: Endangered animals
Polluted water and air, or people destroying the natural habitat, may mean some animals will become extinct.

If we are to stop Earth Abuse, all of us must take the responsibility to help. As a parent, you can model caring for our Earth by being informed about environmental concerns and helping your whole family begin to practice little things that can make a big difference!

PRACTICE...

The Environment

1. Begin a family adventure of caring for our planet. Here are a few examples for each of the six Earth Abuses:

Air Pollution: Ride your bike or walk to activities instead of taking the car.

Ozone Layer: Read the labels before using aerosol products.

Wasting Water: Keep cold water in the refrigerator rather than letting the faucet run until the water is cold, turn water off while brushing your teeth.

Wasting Energy: Turn off lights when you don't need them, contact electric and gas companies for lots of energy-saving tips and make a family project of instituting some of them.

Too Much Garbage: Recycle! Refuse to buy products in Styrofoam or plastic packaging.

Endangered Animals: Put up birdhouses and feeders. Maintain them carefully; consistency is vital when wild creatures become dependent on you.

You will find additional ideas in resources written especially for children, such as *50 Simple Things Kids Can Do To Save The Earth*; the Earth Works Group, Andrews & McMeel; Kansas City/New York; 1990. These resources include a wealth of information and strategies that everyone in your family can do easily.

2. Take a trip, a hike or just a drive through nearby areas to see and enjoy God's beautiful world. Look at scenery; collect leaves, rocks, wildflowers or bugs; take lots of pictures. Stop somewhere along the way to talk about the intricate detail and endless variety of our world and offer prayers of thanks and praise to God for giving us such a beautiful and interesting place to live. If you took pictures, make a "Praise Album" to display your record of God's creation.

3. Organize a family or community project to clean up litter, especially in areas where it can endanger animals and fish. Beaches and stream or riverbanks are particularly important. Bring large trash bags and see how many you can fill. Then end the day doing something fun together as a family or group.

The Environment

Lesson 1 ✓

Our Unique Planet

Aim: That your students will thank God for creating, maintaining, and giving the earth to us
Scripture: Psalm 104:1-31
Unit Verse: It is required that those who have been given a trust must prove faithful. I Corinthians 4:2
Unit Affirmation: I CAN ENJOY LIVING IN MY WORLD!

✓ Planning Ahead

1. Photocopy activity sheets (pages 59 and 60)—one for each student.
2. Prepare the Unit Affirmation poster by writing across the top of a large poster board, I CAN ENJOY LIVING IN MY WORLD! Under the title, write the numbers 1-4 vertically down the left-hand side.

1 Setting the Stage (5-10 minutes)
WHAT YOU'LL DO
- Prepare a bulletin board background or mural to use for the Unit Verse each week during this unit.

WHAT YOU'LL NEED
- Newsprint, or an attractive paper to use for the Unit bulletin board or mural background
- Purchased bulletin board border strips, or wallpaper or gift wrap to make borders
- Strips of paper for captions
- Yarn
- Magazines or old Sunday school materials that contain pictures and words describing God's creation of the Earth

2 Introducing the Issue (20 minutes)
WHAT YOU'LL DO
- Make a list of the things that make a good environment
- Use an activity sheet to discover how God created our world to be the perfect environment for us to enjoy
- Introduce the Unit Affirmation poster

WHAT YOU'LL NEED
- "It's the Best!" Activity Sheet (page 59)
- Unit Affirmation poster

3 Searching the Scriptures (20 minutes)
WHAT YOU'LL DO
- Use an activity sheet to decode a puzzle and notice how our wise God created Earth to sustain life
- Add a picture(s) illustrating God's creation to the Unit bulletin board

WHAT YOU'LL NEED
- Bibles
- "Makin' It Great!" Activity Sheet (page 60)
- Picture(s) of God's creation

4 Living the Lesson (5-10 minutes)
WHAT YOU'LL DO
- Make an acrostic to find ways to thank God for giving Earth to us and rejoice in His gift

WHAT YOU'LL NEED
- Optional: dictionary or thesaurus

Lesson 1

The Environment

✓ Setting the Stage (5-10 minutes)

As your students arrive today, involve them in preparing the background for a bulletin board or mural, which you will add to each week as you study the Unit Verse. Some students can pin or staple the background paper in place, and others can measure and cut strips for the border. Have someone use yarn to divide the board into four sections, one for each lesson in this unit. Ask students to prepare two captions. You will need the unit verse printed out to be used as a title for the whole board, and a smaller caption for today's section, "EARTH—GOD'S GIFT".

As students complete their assignments, ask them to look through the magazines and old Sunday school materials and cut out pictures to represent the seven days of creation (see Genesis 1). **Today we are starting a new unit all about God's gift of giving us our beautiful world in which to live. How can a world be a gift?** As they finish cutting out the pictures, ask them to share their reactions to the phrase, "EARTH—GOD'S GIFT." Save the pictures to use in SEARCHING THE SCRIPTURES.

✓ Introducing the Issue (20 minutes)

You have probably heard the term "environmental concerns" used to talk about taking care of our world. What does the word "environment" mean? (A setting in which all the conditions needed for normal growth and development are provided.) **What are some "environments" you have in your life?** (Your bedroom is an environment set up with all you need for relaxation activities and rest; your school classroom is set up with all you need to learn well; your house is set up with all you need for living comfortably; our city or town is set up with all we need for all our families to live together, such as places to work and play, schools for kids to learn, and police to protect us.)

As kids respond to the next two questions, list their responses on the board. **Environments can be good or bad. What are some characteristics of good environments?** Characteristics of good environments would include: 1) Supplies everything we need to do whatever we are supposed to do in that environment (a bedroom needs a bed, a bathroom needs a bathtub and toilet, a schoolroom needs desks and blackboards. 2) Is comfortable and pleasant (good smells, comfortable furniture, nicely decorated, clean. 3) Is safe (cities have good police departments, schools have rules, homes don't have bare electrical wires.) **What are some characteristics of bad environments?** (Just the opposite of the above list: does not have everything we need, is unpleasant,

The Environment

Lesson 1

uncomfortable, and unsafe. Kids can give specific examples of these in terms of their bedrooms, schoolrooms, neighborhoods, etc.)

> **OPTIONAL:** If you have the time, divide your class into two or three groups and give each one a piece of poster board or other large paper. Tell them that their task is to design the perfect bedroom environment for kids their age. It can be as big and have as much stuff in it as they want. It can even be a bedroom of the future and include things that haven't even been invented yet. Set a time limit, and let them "go to it." When they are finished, let each group describe their environment to the rest of the class.

Distribute copies of the activity sheet, "It's the Best!" (page 59). **Our world is an environment, too. Genesis 1 tells us that God carefully and lovingly prepared a special place for His creation. He paid attention to all the details necessary for making sure it would be a good environment.** To complete the activity sheet, have kids look at the verses in Genesis to see what God created on each of the first five days. As they discover each one, they can draw a picture of it in the blank area. This should be an add-on picture so that when it is finished it will be a picture of the environment God created for us. Stop after day five and refer to your list on the board of the characteristics of a good environment. **So far, how does the world God created for us fulfill these characteristics?** (It had everything that would be needed to sustain life, like air, light, darkness for rest, food and water, and animals for companionship and fun; it was beautiful and comfortable; and it was completely safe.)

Notice that God provided all this before He created human beings. **In a way, God was acting like a loving parent preparing to bring a new baby home from the hospital. What do parents do to prepare an environment for their new child?** (They set up a place as a nursery where the baby can sleep comfortably; they stock up with baby food, diapers, clothes and toys so the baby can have all its needs cared for comfortably.) **That is a perfect picture of what God did when He created the world. When all was ready, He created humans and placed them in His beautiful world.** Have kids finish their sheets by drawing Adam and Eve into their pictures.

Display the Unit Affirmation poster and have the kids read the Affirmation aloud together. **During this unit we will discover that we can enjoy living in our world when we take the time to work at making it a good place to be. We can begin today by celebrating the great gift God gave us when He created our beautiful planet.** Write "by thanking God for giving us our beautiful Earth" on the first line. **Now let's look at a psalm that will help us do that.**

55

Lesson 1

The Environment

✓ Searching the Scriptures (20 minutes)

Start this section by having students close their eyes and picture in their minds the most beautiful place they have ever been or would like to visit. As kids' eyes are closed, ask thought questions to help them imagine this place. **What time of day is it—day or night? What do you hear—birds, water running? What do you smell—flowers, fruit, new-mown hay? What does your body feel—warm breezes, sea spray, sunshine?** Allow students to share briefly. Help them to see that as beautiful as this place might be, the perfect world God created was even more beautiful.

Because God created the Earth without the curse of sin upon it, there were no weeds, death, or decay. Let's find out what it was it like. Distribute copies of the activity sheet "Makin' It Great!" (page 60). Ask someone to read the directions aloud. Give small groups three or four of the sentences to complete and then have each group share its answers with the rest of the class. After decoding the words, have students turn to Psalm 104:10-31. Discuss God's work of creation as you check the answers for this exercise. Answers are: springs, earth, grass, plants, oil, trees, nests, mountains, moon, darkness, sea, food, breath, renews, rejoices.

What do these verses tell us about who is in control of our world? (God is in control.) **How does this make you feel?** (Kids will probably find that these things give them a sense of security.) **What provisions has God made for the basic needs of every living thing?** (He gives them food and water, light for working and growing times, darkness for rest.)

Have someone read Genesis 1:26-29. **To whom did God give the earth?** (Adam and Eve originally, now to all people.) **Look at Psalm 104:20-23. What special arrangement did God make to protect people and animals?** Point out that the majority of dangerous wild animals hunt at night when people are at rest. Then when people are at work outside, these animals are at rest in their dens. God made it so that they wouldn't endanger each other!

God created individual things so that they are not only cared for themselves but also help to take care of each other. Where in this psalm can you find some evidence of that? Verses 16 and 17 show how God gives trees water. Trees in turn provide shelter for the birds. In verses 14 and 15 we see how people take care of plants, which in turn provide food, drink, and other helps for people and animals. Explain that in the hot desert air where the psalmist lived, people's skin and hair dried out. Olive oil was a necessity to maintain moisture. It was the skin lotion of that day.

Have someone read Psalm 104:29. **What would happen if God stopped caring for Earth and its inhabitants?** (There would be great fear and even-

The Environment

Lesson 1

tually death for everything.) Point out that God didn't simply create the world and then abandon it. He continues to take care of His creation. **What evidence can you find in this psalm that God continues to take care of the earth?** Verse 30 tells us that He continues to renew the face of the earth.

Ask someone to read Colossians 1:16, 17. **What does verse 17 say about God's maintenance of the earth today?** (Christ holds everything together.) Point out that this includes all of our universe. When we follow His directions for caring for Earth, He makes things run smoothly like a beautifully designed machine. Emphasize that if God has such total control and endless power over all creation, we can trust Him to handle our lives.

> **OPTIONAL:** If time permits, let your kids do some creative thinking by asking some "what if" questions throughout this lesson. **If you had helped God when He created the world, what would Earth look like? What color would you have made the grass and sky? What animals would you have created? Would you have made people differently?** Allow a few minutes for fun discussion.

Have the class read the Unit Verse together from I Corinthians 4:2. "It is required that those who have been given a trust must prove faithful." **What is the trust God has given us?** (Take care of Earth, our environment.) Point out that when the Lord created the world it was made perfectly. Everything grew and reproduced the way it was supposed to do. Plants, animals, and people lived together in complete harmony with God providing everything needed. This was and still is God's intention for His creation.

As we study throughout this unit we are going to form an "E" team. Explain that this team will be involved in learning about, appreciating, and caring for the Earth and our environment. Have your students help you choose some pictures from those cut out in SETTING THE STAGE. Attach these to the bulletin board or mural in the section with the heading, "EARTH—GOD'S GIFT." If possible, the pictures should illustrate the harmony of all living things.

✓ Living the Lesson (5-10 minutes)

Ask students to read Psalm 104:31 together. **This is a type of thank-You prayer from the psalm writer that expresses his appreciation for God's gift of the Earth to him.** Distribute the paper, pencils, and drawing supplies. Have students write "THANK YOU, GOD" vertically and make an acrostic out of it. They can list one thing from nature that they rejoice in and appreciate for each letter of this phrase. A dictionary or thesaurus may be helpful in this

Lesson 1

The Environment

activity. A sample acrostic is:
- **T**winkling stars
- **H**ollyhocks
- **A**ardvarks
- **N**ight
- **K**angaroos
- **Y**ellowstone Falls
- **O**rioles
- **U**nique snowflakes
- **G**oldfinches
- **O**ranges
- **D**ogs

Look over your acrostic list. Compare it with some of the things Psalm 104 listed. Point out that this psalm writer listed fearful things such as hunting lions and dark nights as well as beautiful birds and mountains. **Can we be thankful for things that seem scary or strange as well as those that are beautiful?** (Yes.) **Why?** (Because we know that God has a purpose for them and is in control of all of them.) **How can we show our thanks to God for all that He has created?** Guide your students to see that as we care for and protect God's creations we display appreciation to Him. Allow volunteers to briefly share how they would care for some of the items on their list. If time permits, kids can illustrate their acrostics.

Close by singing one verse of some song about creation such as "He's Got the Whole World in His Hands" or "Great Is Thy Faithfulness." You might also ask volunteers to pray and thank God for His gift of Earth.

It's the Best!

When God created the world, He made it the very best possible environment for His creation to live in. Look up the following verses in Genesis 1 to discover what God created on each day. Then draw a picture that includes each new creation and see how the Earth became a beautiful place to live.

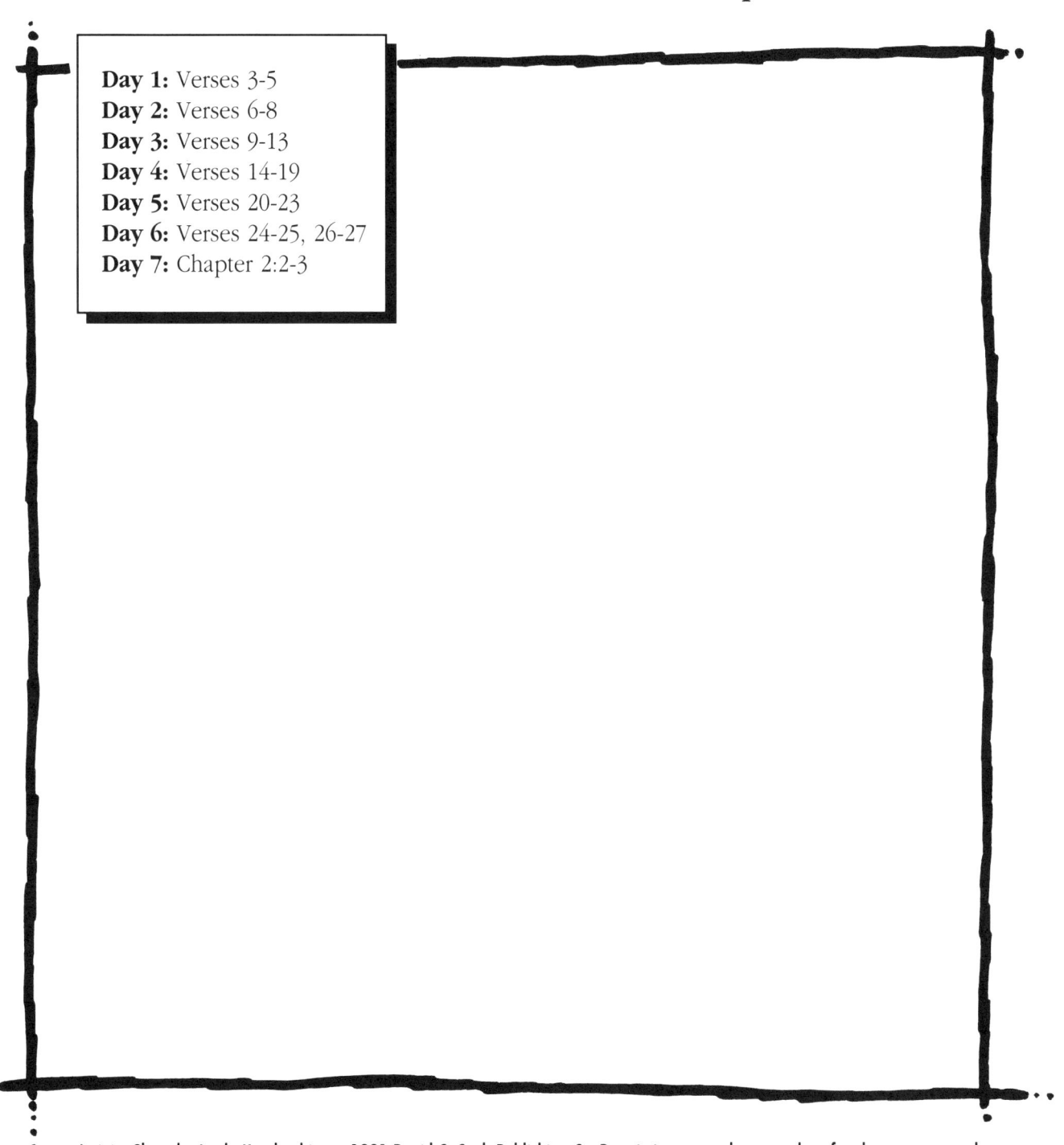

Day 1: Verses 3-5
Day 2: Verses 6-8
Day 3: Verses 9-13
Day 4: Verses 14-19
Day 5: Verses 20-23
Day 6: Verses 24-25, 26-27
Day 7: Chapter 2:2-3

Activity Sheet by Linda Kondracki © 1991 David C. Cook Publishing Co. Permission granted to reproduce for classroom use only.

Makin' It Great!

Use the code to discover some interesting things about our world. After you have finished, turn to Psalm 104:10-31 to check your answers. This psalm is a beautiful picture of God's creation and care for the earth.

CODE: A=(becomes)F B=G C=H D=I E=K F=L G=M H=N I=O J=P K=R L=S
M=T N=U O=V P=W Q=Y R=A S=B X=C T=D U=E Z=J

1. _____ quench the thirst of all the beasts of the field.
   L J K D H B L
2. The _____ is satisfied by the fruit of God's work.
   U R K M C
3. God makes _____ grow for the cattle.
   B K R L L
4. _____ give food from the earth for people.
   J F R H M L
5. In the dry desert _____ helps protect the faces of people.
   I D F
6. The Lord planted and waters the _____ .
   M K U U L
7. In turn they provide places for _____ for the birds.
   H U L M L
8. _____ are a refuge for the wild goats and rock badgers.
   G I N H M R D H L
9. We mark off the seasons by watching the _____.
   G I I H
10. When it is night and there is _____, the wild animals such as lions seek their food from God.   **T R K E H U L L**
11. There are creatures beyond number in the vast and spacious _____.
    L U R
12. All living things look to God to give them their _____ at the proper time.
    A I I T
13. When the Lord takes away their _____, they die.
    S K U R M C
14. God has created the earth and also _____ its face.
    K U H U P L
15. He _____ in His works.
    K U Z I D X U L

Activity Sheet by Bev Gundersen © 1991 David C. Cook Publishing Co. Permission granted to reproduce for classroom use only.

The Environment

Lesson 2 ✓

A World Full of Wonder

Aim: That your students will develop an appreciation for the diversity found in God's creation
Scripture: Genesis 1:1-27; Selected Scriptures
Unit Verse: It is required that those who have been given a trust must prove faithful. I Corinthians 4:2
Unit Affirmation: I CAN ENJOY LIVING IN MY WORLD!

✓ Planning Ahead

1. Photocopy Activity Sheets (pages 67 and 68)—one for each student.
2. Make cards for a game "What Am I?" by printing one card for each student. On each 3" x 5" card, write the name of something from God's creation. Use a wide variety of items, such as whale, lion, flower, mountain, river, bear, dandelion, camel, spider, lizard, turtle, cactus.
3. Write these Bible references on separate pieces of paper: Romans 1:20-22; Romans 1:25; I John 4:8.
4. Make a caption "GOD'S CREATIONS" to add to the Unit Bulletin Board or Mural.
5. Cut out a few pictures showing a variety of God's creations from nature.

1 Setting the Stage (5-10 minutes)
WHAT YOU'LL DO

- Play "What Am I?" to discover the variety of items in God's creation

WHAT YOU'LL NEED

- Cards for "What Am I?"

2 Introducing the Issue (20 minutes)
WHAT YOU'LL DO

- Use an activity sheet to explore the diversity found in creation
- Add a phrase to the Unit Affirmation poster

WHAT YOU'LL NEED

- "God's Variety Show" Activity Sheet (page 67)
- Unit Affirmation poster

3 Searching the Scriptures (20 minutes)
WHAT YOU'LL DO

- Use an activity sheet to become Environmental Detectives and take a look at the variety of God's creation mentioned in Scripture
- Add a picture(s) of the variety of God's creation and a caption to the Unit bulletin board or mural

WHAT YOU'LL NEED

- Bibles
- "From God with Love" Activity Sheet (page 68)
- A picture representing the diversity in God's creation and caption "GOD'S CREATIONS"
- OPTIONAL: magnifying glass, microscope

4 Living the Lesson (5-10 minutes)
WHAT YOU'LL DO

- Make a montage to express appreciation for the variety and creativity seen in creation

WHAT YOU'LL NEED

- Seed catalogs and magazines that contain pictures of plants, animals, or other creations in nature

Lesson 2

The Environment

✓ Setting the Stage (5-10 minutes)

As each student arrives today, tape a 3" x 5" card to his or her back, without telling what the card says. To play "Who Am I?", each student is to interact with other class members to find out what item of God's creation is written on the card. The rules are: 1) They can only ask questions that can be answered with YES or NO, and 2) they can only ask two questions of any one person (unless they have asked two questions of everyone and still don't know what is on their card). After all identities have been discovered, ask the students to introduce themselves to the group as the item written on the card. **All these are examples of things God has created, and this is just a tiny part of what's in our world. Just think about how different each of these things is! Today we want to talk about how awesome the variety of things God placed in our world really is!**

✓ Introducing the Issue (20 minutes)

Have you ever heard the phrase, "Variety is the Spice of Life"? What do you think it means? (Life would be very boring if everything were the same.) **Imagine living in a world that looked like this: there is only one color — everything is RED; there is only one kind of animal — lions (no dogs or cats!); all the people looked exactly alike. Fortunately, God did not give us that kind of world. Instead, He placed so much variety in it that we could never see everything in our world if we spent our whole lives trying!**

Distribute copies of the activity sheet "God's Variety Show" (page 67). God not only used variety in the number of different things He created in our world, He also used variety in what they would look like, feel like, sound like and taste like. He gave us many wonderful things to tantalize all of our five senses! Brainstorm ideas and complete the activity sheet together.

Use the following exercises to explore the variety in God's creation.

SIZE. Have your students stand up and go to an area of the room where they can move around a bit. Have them close their eyes and keep them closed as they form a line according to their height. When they are standing in a straight line with the tallest on one end and the shortest on the other, they can open their eyes and return to their seats. **God not only made people to come in various sizes, His whole creation runs from the very, very small to the very, very large!**

The Environment

Lesson 2

COLOR. Give the class one minute to silently look around the room and make a list of all the colors seen. At the end of the minute, compare lists and recognize the student with the longest list. **Color is one of the most beautiful parts of God's creation! Imagine a world all in black and white! What is your favorite color?** Let kids respond, and then share the colorful parts of God's creation that they like the most, such as rainbows, a field of flowers, or butterflies.

SHAPE. Go around the class asking each student to name one shape they see in the room, such as tall, wide, square, circle, pear-shaped, triangle, or anything else they can name! Then, go around one more time asking them to give examples of the variety of shapes found in God's creation. (Trees are tall and skinny, elephants are big and round pebbles are small and round, eggs are oval.)

TEXTURE. What does "texture" mean? (The way things feel, such as rough, smooth, grainy, sharp, soft, hard.) Give the class one minute to walk around the room and touch as many different textures in the room as they can find (different kinds of cloth, table tops, water, carpet, walls, windows). **What are some examples of the way God used texture in His creation?** Let the kids brainstorm ideas, such as tree bark (rough), rose thorns (sharp), water (liquid), sand (grainy), rock (hard or smooth), grass (soft).

SOUND. Ask for two volunteers to come forward. Seat one on a chair with his or her eyes closed. Place a set of keys under the chair. The other volunteer must stand about five yards behind the chair, sneak up and take the keys out from under the chair and return to the starting point. The trick is this: any time the child on the chair hears the other approaching or taking the keys, she or he may turn around and say "I hear you!" and the game is over. You can repeat this activity with new volunteers as long as you have time available. **As you can see, sounds are very important to us. They serve many purposes, such as protection, communication, and relaxation. What are your favorite sounds?** Let the kids share, and then brainstorm examples of how God used variety in sounds in His creation: everything from the tiny sound of a rabbit or mouse, to the mighty roar of a lion. He also created relaxing sounds like gentle rain and the song of a bird.

Display the Unit Affirmation poster and read the Affirmation aloud together. Ask kids to think of a phrase to add to the second line. A possibility might be, "by observing all the variety in it." **So far, we have seen just a little of the variety in God's creation. Now let's take a closer look at Genesis 1 and see what else we can discover about God's creation.**

63

Lesson 2

The Environment

✓ Searching the Scriptures (20 minutes)

During this lesson students will be looking up several Bible passages. Give three students the papers with the references written on them, have them look up the verses and be prepared to read them.

Have students turn to Genesis 1:1-27 in their Bibles. This is a familiar passage to many Junior-age kids, but in the light of secular teachings that question the truth of an omnipotent God creating the world, we need to look at it again and point out some special things found in this story.

Have someone read aloud verse one. **Who does the Bible say created the earth?** (God.) The questions about Earth's creation are not new. Even in biblical times people wondered how it all began and devised theories about it. Ask the people who looked up Romans 1:20-22 and Romans 1:25 to read them. **What did people refuse to do?** (Glorify God or thank Him for Earth.) **What did they worship instead of God?** (The things He made.) **What are God's thoughts about those who refuse to accept the truth about the world's creation?** (They are foolish.)

Scientists who are followers of Jesus have several different theories of how God created the world. Some believe He made it in seven twenty-four hour days. Some believe that it was during seven twenty-four hour days that God revealed what He had done. While still others think the "days" were seven indefinite periods of time. The exact length of time is not the important thing. The essential truth is that God did make it! **Why do you think God created the Earth?** Allow kids to ponder this awhile. **God didn't need to make our world. He made it because He wanted to.** Ask the person who looked up I John 4:8 to read it aloud. **How is God described here?** (God is love.) Stress that God chose to create the world because He wanted to express His love to someone. Have someone read aloud Genesis 1:27. **To whom did God express His love?** (People.)

Not only did God choose to make the world but when He did so He created it in an orderly manner. Have students read Genesis 1:2. **What was the earth like when God began it?** (Formless and empty.) Guide students in seeing that the second and third days of creation were spent giving form to the universe surrounding the earth. Then during the next three days God filled the earth with living creatures. **God planned out everything in perfect detail. He waited until there was light before creating plants which would need it to grow. He made plants before He fashioned the animals and people who would need those plants for food.**

Help your students realize that when God made the world He considered

The Environment

Lesson 2

people as His crowning achievement. They were the direct object of His love and could communicate directly with Him. In His eyes we have a valuable place far above all His other earthly creations.

We can learn several things about God from this Scripture passage. God likes to make things. He is imaginative and artistic. He is the eternal Creator who has always existed. Not only is He the Creator, but He also allows us to have a part with Him in the creative joy of working with things such as gardens.

What did God think about the Earth and all the other things He had made? (They were good.) Highlight the fact that the Bible says God made everything exactly the way He wanted it. **As active members of the "E" team, you are going to be Environmental Detectives today.** Distribute copies of the activity sheet "From God with Love" (page 68). Ask a student to read the directions.

Divide your class into five teams. Their assignment is to discover specific creations mentioned in Scripture. Be alert to kids who may not be familiar with the Bible and team them up with others who can help them out. Assign one section to each team. While students are working on this activity, circulate among the teams so that you can offer any necessary help. List all the discoveries of this activity on a large sheet of paper and have everyone finish the activity sheet with the discoveries of the other teams.

Answers are: (1) hawk, eagle; fish; lilies; lions; horses, sheep, goats, cattle, donkeys; bear. (2) gnat, camel; olive leaf, dove; cucumbers, melons, leeks, onions, garlic; bees, thorns; ant; frogs. (3) rooster (cock); cedar, aloes; vipers, spiders; quail; deer; snakes, scorpions. (4) ravens; wheat, barley, beans, lentils; apples; locusts; bull, ox; boars. (5) pine, fir, cypress; thorns, thistles; mustard; lizard; leopard; wolf, sheep.

Discuss the results of the Bible search. **Did the variety of creations mentioned in the Bible surprise you? Why do you think God made the world the way He did? Why do you think He included things we often regard as strange or irritations such as locusts and gnats?** Guide kids to see and appreciate the beauty and humor in even the oddest of these items.

> **OPTIONAL:** If you have time, provide the opportunity for students to develop this appreciation by using a magnifying glass or microscope to examine common items. Exploring a human hair in this way can be an adventure into the unknown!

Have students say I Corinthians 4:2 together. **God made our world very thoughtfully. He was happy with it and enjoyed everything He had**

Lesson 2

The Environment

made. As its ruler He lovingly cared for it. Have someone read Genesis 1:26 aloud. **Who did God put in charge of all His creations?** (People.) **What do you think God wants us to do with that responsibility?** (He wants us to enjoy the creation, take care of the creation, and thank God for His creation.)

Students can help put up the pictures and heading on today's section of the Unit bulletin board or mural, "GOD'S CREATIONS."

✓ Living the Lesson (5-10 minutes)

Hand out the paper, glue, seed catalogs and magazines. Have students make individual montages of their favorite animals, birds, fish, plants or scenery from these materials. To make the montage, they will tear out pictures and words that illustrate their choice, arrange, and glue them on the paper. While they are doing this, focus the conversation on questions such as: **Why are the items you chose special to you? What do you like best about them? How can we learn to appreciate everything in God's creation? Where is a good place to see them? When is a good time to tell God "thank You" for His nature gifts to us?** Allow time for students to share their creations with the rest of the class. Ask volunteers to thank God briefly for the wonderful diversity of His creations.

God's Variety Show!

When God created the world, He used an endless amount of variety not only in WHAT He created, but in HOW He created the things He placed in it. Write or draw examples of God's variety in the spaces below.

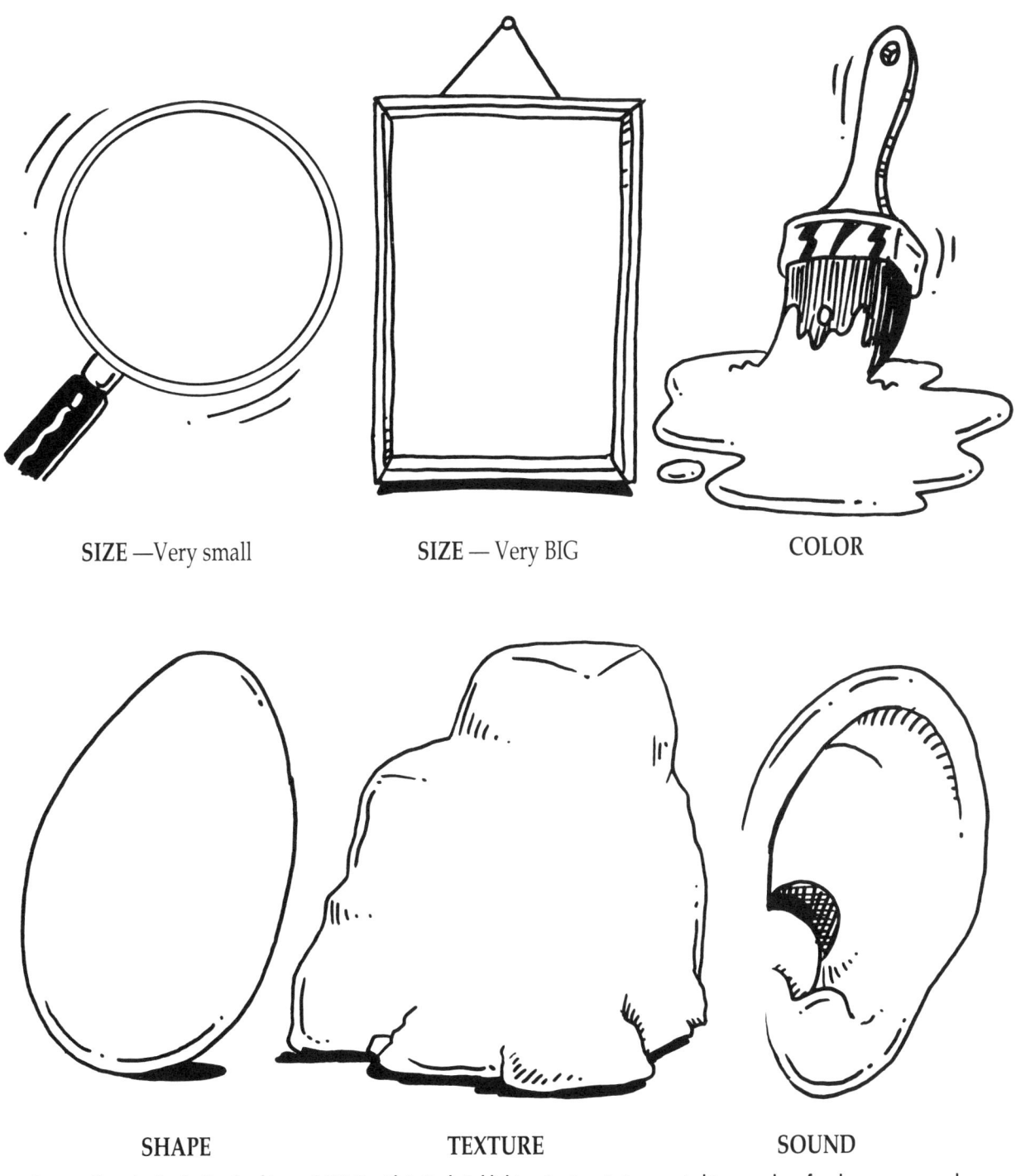

SIZE —Very small   **SIZE** — Very BIG   **COLOR**

SHAPE   **TEXTURE**   **SOUND**

Activity Sheet by Linda Kondracki © 1991 David C. Cook Publishing Co. Permission granted to reproduce for classroom use only.

From God with Love

God made an almost endless variety of living things when He made Earth. Many of the things He made are mentioned in the Bible. As good detectives, follow the clues and discover the creations they report.

(SECTION ONE)
- Job 39:26, 27 _____
- Matthew 17:27 _____
- Luke 12:27 _____
- Psalm 34:10 _____
- Genesis 47:17 _____
- Proverbs 17:12 _____

(SECTION TWO)
- Matthew 23:24 _____
- Genesis 8:11 _____
- Numbers 11:4-6 _____
- Psalm 118:12 _____
- Proverbs 6:6 _____
- Exodus 8:2 _____

(SECTION THREE)
- Mark 14:72 _____
- Numbers 24:6 _____
- Isaiah 59:5 _____
- Numbers 11:31 _____
- Psalm 42:1 _____
- Deuteronomy 8:15 _____

(SECTION FOUR)
- Luke 12:24 _____
- II Samuel 17:28, 29 _____
- Proverbs 25:11 _____
- Joel 1:4 _____
- Deuteronomy 33:17 _____
- Psalm 80:13 _____

(SECTION FIVE)
- Isaiah 60:13 _____
- Genesis 3:18 _____
- Matthew 13:31 _____
- Proverbs 30:28 _____
- Jeremiah 13:23 _____
- John 10:12 _____

Activity Sheet by Bev Gundersen © 1991 David C. Cook Publishing Co. Permission granted to reproduce for classroom use only.

The Environment

Lesson 3

Caretakers of Earth

Aim: That your students will know that God appointed people to become caretakers of the earth and we are accountable to God for protecting it.

Scripture: Genesis 2:2-9, 15, 18-23; Leviticus 25:1-7, 18-22

Unit Verse: It is required that those who have been given a trust must prove faithful. I Corinthians 4:2

Unit Affirmation: I CAN ENJOY LIVING IN MY WORLD!

✓ Planning Ahead

1. Photocopy Activity Sheets (pages 75 and 76)—one for each student.
2. Make one set of 32 cards for every three to four students for a matching game. For each set, make duplicate (matching) cards of the following. Use the names of eight things in God's creation (tulips, horse, river, lion,) and eight names of things man has created (cars, plastic, aluminum, freeways).
3. Prepare an "earthkeeping" advertisement as described in SEARCHING THE SCRIPTURES.
4. Make a caption "EARTHKEEPERS" to add to the Unit Bulletin Board or Mural.
5. Cut out a few pictures showing people planting trees, plants, or helping with natural habitats.

1 Setting the Stage (5-10 minutes)
WHAT YOU'LL DO
- Play a matching game to see the difference between things God has created and things man has created

WHAT YOU'LL NEED
- Sets of matching cards

2 Introducing the Issue (20 minutes)
WHAT YOU'LL DO
- See an object lesson to discuss how easy it is to abuse the Earth's environment
- Use an activity sheet to take ownership of fighting Earth Abuse
- Add a phrase to the Unit Affirmation poster

WHAT YOU'LL NEED
- One penny for each student
- "Stop Earth Abuse — Join the "E" Team!" Activity Sheet (page 75)
- Clear contact paper or lamination film, hole punch, yarn or string
- Unit Affirmation poster

3 Searching the Scriptures (20 minutes)
WHAT YOU'LL DO
- Use an activity sheet and read a skit to emphasize how people are accountable to God for protecting and saving the Earth
- Look at some little things that can cause big problems in the environment
- Add a picture of people helping and a caption to the Unit bulletin board or mural

WHAT YOU'LL NEED
- Bibles
- "Earthshaking News" Activity Sheet (page 76)
- Balloon, Styrofoam cup, aluminum pop can
- A picture of people helping and caption "EARTHKEEPERS"

4 Living the Lesson (5-10 minutes)
WHAT YOU'LL DO
- Do a self-rating to examine ways to influence the environment and determine what needs to be done differently

WHAT YOU'LL NEED
- Paper, pencils

Lesson 3

The Environment

✓ Setting the Stage (5-10 minutes)

As students arrive today, distribute the match-game cards (See PLANNING AHEAD.), one set to every three or four kids. To play, students mix-up the cards and then spread them out face down on the table creating five or six rows of cards. Players take turns turning over two cards at a time, trying to make a match. If they turn over a match, they can remove the cards and keep them. If the cards do not match, they turn them face down again and the next player takes a turn. Continue until all matches have been made and removed from the table. Now have kids look at all the cards and tell you what they observe about them. Let them keep guessing until someone observes that there are things God created and things man created. **In the past few weeks we have been talking about all the wonderful things God has created. Today we will talk about some of the things man has created and how they affect the environment.**

✓ Introducing the Issue (20 minutes)

Your students have most likely studied environmental concerns in school. Ask them to share with you what they already know about things that endanger the earth's environment. Make a list of these things on the board. Items to include are: Spray cans, Styrofoam and similar plastics that don't decompose, wasting water, wasting energy, polluting the water, too much garbage and litter. **It's hard to imagine that we could ever run out of the Earth's resources, or hurt the Earth by anything we do. It seems so big, we don't really think about it much. We throw away garbage and someone comes and gets it and it's gone. We don't think about where it goes or just how much of it there is! We turn on the faucet and there's always water there. Let's see if we can think about it in another way.**

Take a penny out of your pocket. **This is just one little penny. It doesn't mean much to me, because it is so small. Does anyone want it?** Give the penny to someone in your class. **Well, that doesn't seem fair. I should give a penny to everyone here.** Give a penny to everyone. **That didn't cost me very much. But what if I had to give a penny to everyone in our church? How much would that cost?** Calculate the amount together. **Now what if I had to give just one little penny to everyone in our state? How much would that cost?** Calculate the amount. **And what if I gave a penny to everyone on earth?** (That would cost about $60 million dollars!) **In the same**

The Environment

Lesson 3

way, one wasted gallon of water, or one extra aluminum can thrown in the trash may seem like a very little thing to you. But multiply that by the billions of people living on Earth and it all adds up to a big problem!

Distribute copies of the activity sheet, "Stop Earth Abuse — Join the E Team!" (page 75). **Whenever we go on treating the Earth as if it will last forever, or tell ourselves that "this one little thing won't make a difference," we are committing "Earth Abuse". By joining the E Team, we can become "Earth Abuse Arresters."** (Be sure kids understand the play on words, the word "arrest" means to stop something or someone. By stopping behaviors that contribute to earth abuse, we are "arresting" [stopping] the destruction of our planet.) Work together to fill in the names of the "Six Most Wanted Earth Abusers." Discuss the following information about each abuse.

1: Air Polluters — When factories and cars keep pouring harmful gases into the air, it becomes unsafe for people and animals to breathe.

2: Ozone Layer Harmers — Gases used in the cooling units of air conditioners and refrigerators, plastic foam and some aerosol cans are damaging the layer of ozone that protects us from harmful rays from the sun. If this continues, people on earth could die from over exposure to the sun.

3: Water Wasters — The earth has the same amount of water no matter how many people live on it. With more people on earth than ever before, we have to use less to be sure there is enough for everyone.

4: Energy Wasters — The factories that burn coal and oil to generate electricity pollute the air; the less energy we use, the less they have to run. Using lots of batteries (as we do!) is also a problem; when we throw them away they pollute the earth.

5: Garbage Makers — When garbage is thrown away, it is taken to landfills and buried. The idea is it will rot and become part of the earth again. However, so much of our garbage is plastics, aluminum and glass that doesn't rot, and our landfills are overflowing!

6: Animal Endangerers — Polluted water or air, or people destroying an animal's natural habitat, may mean some animals will become extinct.

Now give the kids time to fill in the ID cards and color the armband. Let them cut these out and cover them with clear contact paper. Punch holes in the ends of the armbands and use string or yarn to tie onto the upper arm.

Display the Unit Affirmation poster and read the Affirmation aloud together. Let the kids think of a phrase to add to the third line today. One possibility might be, "when I do my best to take care of it." **Taking good care of the earth is not only a smart thing to do, it is a responsibility God has given to all of us who live on it. Let's see what the Bible has to say about that.**

Lesson 3

The Environment

☑ Searching the Scriptures (20 minutes)

Before class, print the following advertisement on a large sheet of poster board.

"Help Wanted—People to be Earthkeepers. Must be responsible, hard workers, good planners and organizers. Benefits are long-range. Life insurance provided according to degree of success achieved. If interested, please call me at E-A-R-T-H any time. I'm always there. An equal opportunity employer."

Display this sign. **What do you think this ad means?** After students have expressed their thoughts have someone read Genesis 1:28. **After God had made this beautiful world He made people and gave them a special privilege. What did authority did God give people?** (To subdue the earth and rule over it.) **What do you think "to subdue" the earth means?** Guide your students to see that although the word "subdue" sometimes means "to bring something under control," it isn't a permit for exploitation. It is also an agricultural term meaning "to cultivate land."

Ask students to turn to Genesis 2:4-9 and quickly look it over. Explain that this is basically a repetition of the Creation story found in Genesis 1. **Where did God put the man He had formed?** (In the Garden of Eden.) Ask a student to read verse 15 aloud. **Why did God put the man in the garden?** (To work it and take care of it.) Point out this work was given by God and is not a result of sin or God's curse on the world. At this time there were no weeds, droughts, or frosts. The work God gave Adam and Eve was pleasurable and brought joy to them and honor to God.

Distribute copies of the activity sheet "Earthshaking News" (page 76). Choose four people to read the parts of Kid Toppel, Adam, Eve, and Moses. **In the drama, how did Adam link together the authority he had from God with the job God assigned him?** (He said he thought God's intention was for people to be concerned about the earth and care for it like God did.) **Eve said in the skit that every evening she and Adam walked and talked with God. What did she say they talked about?** (How to help and protect God's creations.)

Have someone read aloud Genesis 2:2, 3. Ask another person to read Leviticus 25:4. **What similarities do you see between these two passages?** (Both use the number seven, involve a rest period, are commanded by God to be kept special in His honor.) **In the drama what did Moses say would be the result of following God's rule about conserving the land the seventh year?** (God promised they would have enough food from the sixth year to last them through the ninth year.)

The Environment

Lesson 3

How does the attitude many people have today about using Earth's resources compare with that expressed by Moses in the drama? Many people feel that the earth's resources are here to be used up. There is little or no thought about their ultimate destruction. The idea of giving the land a year of rest is unfamiliar to those who carelessly misuse resources to satisfy their own selfish desires. In contrast, people who desire to obey and honor God realize that they are to be caretakers of Earth and to do all they can to conserve and protect it.

Ask a person to read Leviticus 25:18, 19 aloud. **What does God ask us to do?** (Follow His orders and obey His laws.) **What promise does He give us if we do this?** (We will live safely in the land, we will have all the food we need.) **Do you think God is still able to keep His promises?** (Yes.)

Help students see that because of the seriousness of our environmental problems it is important for them to take action on the matter of how they affect the earth. Many choices may seem small but have wide-spread consequences. Display the balloon, Styrofoam cup, and aluminum can. **What do these items have in common?** Several things could be mentioned: they are familiar to kids, often left as litter, not very impressive-looking or expensive. The most important thing is that they are all hazardous to the environment.

Balloons can float away and sea creatures eat them thinking they are food. Later this can kill them. Silver metallic balloons can get caught on power lines and cause outages affecting thousands of people.

Styrofoam becomes permanent garbage. When burned it releases pollutants which can damage the ozone layer protecting the earth from hazardous rays. If animals or sea creatures eat Styrofoam, the plastic may cause them to die.

Aluminum cans may take over 200 years to decompose. Deer and other animals can cut their tongues on jagged edges of partly opened cans.

Have students repeat the Unit Verse, I Corinthians 4:2, together. **What trust has God given to us?** (To take care of the earth.) **How can we be faithful in keeping that trust?** (By doing whatever we can to protect and conserve God's creations.) Repeat the verse, inserting "Earth" for "a trust." Students can help you choose a picture from those you brought to go with the caption "EARTHKEEPERS." Place these items on the Unit bulletin board or mural.

✓ Living the Lesson (5-10 minutes)

Let's look at some ways that you influence the environment every day. Distribute paper and pencils. Explain that students are going to rate themselves as to how they affect the world around them. Have them number

73

Lesson 3

The Environment

from one to ten vertically down the left side of their papers.

They will draw a pictures after each number to indicate their answers. Use this code for your answers: Draw a mountaintop if this is something you do all the time; draw a little hill if you do this most of the time, draw flatlands with no highs or lows if you do this sometimes; draw a swamp—far below hope and equal to the pits—if you need to change.

Read each question aloud and allow time to draw the answers. Encourage them to be as honest as possible and remind them their answers are strictly private.

Do you:

1. collect and recycle soft-drink cans?
2. use rechargeable batteries?
3. pick up your own litter?
4. turn the water off while you brush your teeth?
5. buy and use recycled paper?
6. keep a bottle of drinking water in the refrigerator instead of letting it run from the faucet until it is cold?
7. ever plant a tree?
8. turn out lights when you don't need them?

These are only a few common things kids can do to help care for the environment. Allow time for students to look over their answers. Discuss them briefly: **What happens if you don't do these things?** Focus on how individuals can positively influence their world. **What do you need to do differently? What other things might you do to help care for Earth?**

There are four basic areas we all need to work at: waste, pollution, buying, information. When we are serious about them we begin to fill our roles of Earthkeepers and honor God.

Sing a verse of "This Is My Father's World." Close with prayer.

Stop Earth Abuse! Join the "E" Team!

Stopping earth abuse is everyone's business. Fill out the "Six Most Wanted" list and think of things you can do to stop each one. Then fill in the ID card and armband, cut out all three pieces and cover them with clear adhesive paper. To wear the armband, punch holes in each end, attach string or yarn and tie it to your arm.

"E" Team ID Card

Name _____
Grade _____ School _____
The above named is an official member of the Environmental Team, dedicated to stopping Earth Abuse wherever possible!

Signed _____ Date _____

"E" Team's SIX MOST WANTED EARTH ABUSERS

1. _____
2. _____
3. _____
4. _____
5. _____
6. _____

"E" Team Member... Stopping Earth Abuse

Activity Sheet by Linda Kondracki © 1991 David C. Cook Publishing Co.
Permission granted to reproduce for classroom use only.

75

✓ Earthshaking News

Kid Toppel: Good day. My name is Kid Toppel and this is "Right Line." Today we have three famous guests who will be sharing their views about taking care of our earth. Some people say that we can use our environment any way we desire. Adam, you were the first man in the world. What did God tell you about this?

Adam: God told me to "fill the earth and subdue it. Rule over . . . all the creatures." I don't think that meant for us to take advantage of them, but that God's intention was for us to be concerned about the earth and care for it just like He did. The job He gave me points that out.

Kid Toppel: What job did God give you, Adam?

Adam: He gave me the privilege of taking care of the Garden of Eden. Then He brought me every animal and bird and let me name them. I nearly ran out of ideas!

Kid Toppel: God also made a woman. Eve, you were that woman. What was the Lord's desire for you?

Eve: I was to be Adam's partner. We were responsible for taking care of God's creations. It was a joy to be with the beautiful birds, animals, and plants. Every night God came to talk with us in the garden and He told us how to help and protect everything. Life was wonderful!

Kid Toppel: Thank you, Adam and Eve. After a while people began to neglect this responsibility from God. Then the Lord told Moses how He wanted His people to take care of the earth. Moses, what reminder did God give you?

Moses: He told us to farm and use the land for six years. During the seventh year the land was to rest like God rested after He had created the world. We were not to sow crops or prune our vineyards that year, but instead eat whatever the land grew by itself. The wild animals could eat what grew during that time period.

Kid Toppel: Wouldn't you get hungry that seventh year?

Moses: God promised that if we obeyed Him and faithfully took care of the earth, enough food would grow during the sixth year to feed us all for three years! God is faithful to help you today as He did then if you lovingly care for the earth. This honors Him.

Kid Toppel: There you have it, ladies and gentlemen. Our guests are in agreement that God has appointed us to become caretakers of the earth and we are accountable to Him for protecting and saving it. This is Kid Toppel signing off for "Right Line."

Activity Sheet by Bev Gundersen © 1991 David C. Cook Publishing Co. Permission granted to reproduce for classroom use only.

The Environment

Lesson 4 ✓

United, We Save

Aim: That your students will determine to do something as a group to praise God for our Earth by helping save and protect it
Scripture: Psalm 148:1-13
Unit Verse: It is required that those who have been given a trust must prove faithful. I Corinthians 4:2
Unit Affirmation: I CAN ENJOY LIVING IN MY WORLD!

✓ Planning Ahead

1. Photocopy Activity Sheets (pages 83 and 84)—one for each student.
2. Before class, obtain permission to display today's "E" Team posters in a place where everyone in your church can see them.
3. Make a caption "SAVE THE EARTH" to add to the Unit Bulletin Board or mural.
4. Cut out pictures of groups of people helping to save and protect their environment.

1 Setting the Stage (5-10 minutes)
WHAT YOU'LL DO
- Make "E" Team Strategy Booklets

WHAT YOU'LL NEED
- Two sheets of 8 1/2" x 5 1/2" paper for each child
- Stapler, or long arm or saddle stapler

2 Introducing the Issue (20 minutes)
WHAT YOU'LL DO
- Brainstorm ways to save the earth and write them in the "E" Team Strategy Books
- Use an activity sheet to make "E" Team Awareness Posters
- Finish the Unit Affirmation poster

WHAT YOU'LL NEED
- "E" Team Strategy Booklets made during SETTING THE STAGE
- "STOP EARTH ABUSE!" Activity Sheet (page 83)
- Unit Affirmation poster

3 Searching the Scriptures (20 minutes)
WHAT YOU'LL DO
- Use an activity sheet to praise and honor God for our earth
- Add a picture and caption to the Unit bulletin board or mural

WHAT YOU'LL NEED
- Bibles
- Bag of small candies
- "Praise Song" Activity Sheet (page 84)
- A picture and caption "SAVE THE EARTH"

4 Living the Lesson (5-10 minutes)
WHAT YOU'LL DO
- Observe an illustration of how people can work together to care for the environment
- Find ways to work together with families, community and church to honor God by protecting our earth

WHAT YOU'LL NEED
- Pebble, bowl, small amount of water

Lesson 4

The Environment

✓ Setting the Stage (5-10 minutes)

As your students arrive today, have them make "E" Team Strategy Books for use in INTRODUCING THE ISSUE. To make the booklets, fold two sheets of 8 1/2" x 5 1/2" paper in half and insert one inside the other to make a booklet. If you have a long arm or saddle stapler, use it to staple the books in the middle. If you are using a regular stapler, staple along the left-hand outside edge. Have the kids make the covers by writing "E" TEAM STRATEGY BOOK on the front, and decorating it any way they wish. Then have them write the following headings on the top of each page inside: Arrest Air Pollution by, Arrest Damage to the Ozone Layer by, Arrest Water Wasting by, Arrest Energy Wasting by, Arrest Garbage Making by, and Arrest Animal Endangering by.

Some of you may remember that the "E" Team's 6 Most Wanted Earth Abusers are: Air Polluters, Ozone Layer Harmers, Water Wasters, Energy Wasters, Garbage Makers, and Animal Endangerers. Today we will talk about what we "E" Team members can do to "arrest" these Earth Abusers! Remember, the word "arrest" means "to stop."

✓ Introducing the Issue (20 minutes)

As you discuss the following information, have your students take notes on specific things they can do about earth abuse in their strategy books. **Caring for the earth is a job for everyone. We don't have to feel helpless or powerless because the problem seems too big. Remember, the problem is created by the "little" things we all do, multiplied by the many billions of people on our planet. So, what is the only way we can stop earth abuse?** (By everyone making little changes and doing little things to take better care of the earth.)

What are some things we can do as individuals and groups to arrest air pollution? Let kids brainstorm ideas and write them in their books. Examples: Ride your bike to activities rather than asking parents to drive you; plant a tree (it eats a harmful gas, carbon dioxide). Groups can begin a community campaign to encourage carpools.

What are some things we can do as individuals and groups to arrest damage to the ozone layer? Let kids brainstorm ideas and write them in their books. Examples: Don't use Styrofoam products, keep the air conditioner off unless its *really* hot.

What are some things we can do as individuals and/or groups to arrest the wasting and pollution of our water? Let kids brainstorm ideas

The Environment — Lesson 4

and write them in their books. Examples: Take a short shower and not a bath (using a shower with a flow regulator), don't leave water running while brushing your teeth, keep cold water in the refrigerator rather than letting it run from the faucet until it is cold. Groups can have fun saving our ocean beaches, lakes and streams. Ways to do that are by going out "garbage picking" (garbage pollutes water and kills animals and fish), planting trees along river- and stream banks, and scouting for oil or other harmful substances leaking into the water (these should be reported to the proper authorities).

What are some things we can do as individuals and groups to arrest the wasting of energy? Let kids brainstorm ideas and write them in their books. Examples: Turn off lights when you don't need them, don't keep the refrigerator open while you decide what you want, use rechargeable batteries and solar-powered gadgets when possible. With parents and other family members, inspect your house for ways to make your furnace and hot-water heaters more energy efficient. Contact your electric and gas companies for lots of energy-saving ideas.

What are some things we can do as individuals and groups to arrest the problem of too much garbage? Let kids brainstorm ideas and write them in their books. Examples: Recycle paper, glass and aluminum cans, refuse to use Styrofoam and other products that don't decompose in the earth. Groups can do a lot to encourage recycling in their communities. Think about it together and you'll probably have lots of ideas very quickly!

What are some things we can do as individuals and groups to arrest the problem of endangered animals? Let kids brainstorm ideas and write them in their books. Examples: Plant a garden for small animals and birds to live. Groups can help most by organizing the community to pick up litter in places where animals and fish can be harmed by it.

Distribute copies of the activity sheet "Stop Earth Abuse!" (page 83). **There is one more thing we can do to stop Earth Abuse, and that is to spread the word to others to join the "E" Team and learn ways to care for our Earth. Today we are going to make posters that will tell others in our church how they can help save our planet.** As a class, brainstorm "E" Team slogans that they can put on their posters. Examples: If It Doesn't Rot, It Shouldn't Be Bought! (with a picture of Styrofoam products crossed out); Recycle for Life; Keep the Earth Green — Plant a Tree; Save an Animal - Pick Up Your Litter. Kids can get ideas from the pages of their booklets. Let the kids choose one for their posters, being sure they all choose something different. If possible, have the students display their posters today in different areas around the building. As an alternative, collect them and post them during the week.

Display the Unit Affirmation poster and read it together. Let the kids think of

Lesson 4 — The Environment

a final phrase to add to the fourth line. A possibility might be: "and encourage others to enjoy it, too!" **When we stop to think about it, and look at it, we can see just what a beautiful place God has given us to live. Let's take some time to praise Him for this wonderful world we have!**

✓ Searching the Scriptures (20 minutes)

When God created the world, He made it perfect. None of us were there to see it, but we can get glimpses of what it was like from the Bible. Have people read aloud Job 38:4-7 and Psalm 98:8, 9a. **What do these verses have in common?** (All show nature praising God, their Creator.) **The Bible often shows creation as being capable of praising God as people do with singing voices and clapping hands. These verses show us how God's creations praised and honored Him for the gift of life.** Ask someone to read Isaiah 55:12. **This verse shows creation even rejoicing in the accomplishments of God's people.**

We often talk about praise and honor but many times Junior-age kids don't really comprehend what we mean. **What is praise?** Allow time for kids to think about this. Discuss such things as receiving praise from others, praising someone for an achievement, and other aspects of human praise. **Praise expresses admiration, appreciation, approval and thanks. What is honor?** Allow students to think about and discuss this briefly. **Honor expresses respect, high regard, admiration, and awe.**

Why do you think we should praise and honor God? Help students see that because God has given us life, we want to praise Him. Besides His creations, God also gives us forgiveness and blessings without number. The beautiful earth-home He has given us is a wonderful gift. For that He deserves praise and honor. However, we need to go beyond what God does for us and also praise and honor Him for who He is—the Lord of all things. His love, faithfulness, patience, justice, and forgiveness are beyond our comprehension.

Have students turn to Psalm 148:1-13. Allow students to read over the entire passage silently. **What are some of God's creations that are mentioned here?** Let students name as many as possible. You may want to list these items on the board. Point out that they include heavenly things, weather elements, nature's creatures, and all ages and levels of human society. **What are they all urged to do?** (Praise the Lord.) **What are some of the reasons for doing that?** Talk about things such as God's creation and control, His splendor and power.

The Environment

Lesson 4

Distribute copies of the activity sheet "Praise Song." (page 84) Explain that this is a choral reading adapted from Psalm 148:1-13. It is written like a song that a choir would sing in that it has solos, duets, and whole choir parts. Unlike a song, it doesn't have any music. It is meant to be read. Assign students the solo and duet lines and read the song aloud several times. Change the assignment of parts between readings. This Scripture conveys the feeling of all creation uniting in a beautiful symphony of praise to God.

How can we praise and honor God? (Through prayer, singing, helping others.) Enlarge your student's vision of praise and honor to include taking good care of God's gifts. Hold up a bag of small candy treats. **Let's suppose this bag of treats represents the earth's resources—clean air, water, trees, plants, animals.** Ask a student to come to you. Open the container and give one candy to the student. (Kid's name), **if I give this to you, you can enjoy it. If I give you two or three you will still enjoy them, but what will happen if you eat all the candy in this package?** (Probably get sick.) Point out that the kid won't even enjoy the treat any more. **How do you think I will feel about your using my gift that way?** (Sad, angry, disappointed.) Point out that the giver would feel you didn't appreciate the gift, but selfishly misused it.

What will happen if you take this candy and share it with others? (They can all enjoy it, nobody will get sick.) Have the student give one candy to each kid and return the rest to you. **An abundance is meant to be shared with others. Now we even have some left over to share with others who might come to class later. How do you think I feel about your using my gift this way?** (Happy, pleased, you appreciated the gift, used it wisely to give pleasure to others.)

What will happen if we use up all the earth's resources that God has given us? (They will be gone, we won't really appreciate them, we won't have any left over for future generations.) **How do you think God feels when people misuse and waste Earth?** (Sad, angry, disappointed.) As the object lesson of candy pointed out, God might think we don't really appreciate His gifts or their Giver.

Ask students to say the Unit Verse, I Corinthians 4:2, together. **How do you think we can honor and praise God for His gift of Earth?** (By taking care of it, sharing it with others, not wasting it.) **When we do these things, we can bring about the kind of song of praise that we read together earlier. This is how we can be faithful to the gift of Earth that God has entrusted to us.** Ask kids to help you put up the picture and caption "SAVE THE EARTH"

Lesson 4

The Environment

on the Unit Verse bulletin board or mural.

✓ Living the Lesson (5-10 minutes)

Pour some water into a bowl. Drop a pebble into the water. **What happened?** (Ripples spread out from the pebble.) Explain that when people work together to honor God by protecting Earth the same sort of thing happens. Small deeds spread and reproduce themselves in larger ones. An individual family picking up litter along one mile of roadway seems a small thing, but when others join in, one mile is multiplied to become ten or twenty. The environment improves greatly.

Briefly review the methods kids brainstormed earlier in the lesson. After you have reexamined these techniques, turn your ideas into action.

> **OPTIONAL:** Go on a hike around your building, grounds, or neighborhood. Take note of these kinds of things: What needs doing right here? What can we do as a class? Do we need to stop some practices such as using Styrofoam products or aerosols? Can we start a recycling program of some kind? How about planting trees or gardens? Should we become detectives to discover water, heat, or power leaks or misuses? Do birds or animals need homes or food?

Decide on one "E" Team strategy for the class to do together. Assign teams to work on the various aspects of the project: information and resources, materials, transportation, distribution of waste, publicity. Make definite plans and set dates to carry out your chosen project!

Close by reading the "Praise Song" as a prayer of thanks.

Stop Earth Abuse! ✓

STOP EARTH ABUSE!

The "E" Team Says . . .

Activity Sheet by Linda Kondracki © 1991 David C. Cook Publishing Co. Permission granted to reproduce for classroom use only.

Praise Song

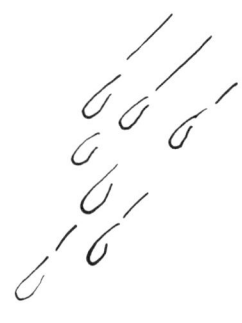

All:	(softly) Praise the Lord.
Girls:	Praise the Lord from the heavens,
	Praise him in the heights above.
Girl Solo:	Praise him, all his angels,
Girl Duet:	Praise him, all his heavenly hosts.
All:	(gathering strength) Praise the Lord.
Girls:	Praise him, sun and moon,
	Praise him, all you shining stars.
	Praise him, you highest heavens,
Boys:	You waters above the skies.
Girl Solo:	Let them praise the name of the Lord,
Boy Solo:	For he commanded and they were created.
Girls:	He set them in place for ever and ever;
	He gave a decree that will never pass away.
All:	(emphatically) Praise the Lord.
Boys:	Praise the Lord from the earth,
	You great sea creatures and all ocean depths,
Boy Solo:	Lightning and hail, snow and clouds,
Boy Duet:	Stormy winds that do his bidding,
	You mountains and all hills,
	Fruit trees and all cedars,
Boys:	Wild animals and all cattle,
	Small creatures and flying birds.
All:	(joyfully) Praise the Lord.
Boy Solo:	Kings of the earth and all nations,
Boy Duet:	You princes and all rulers on earth,
Girl Solo:	Young men and maidens,
Girl Duet:	Old men and children.
Boys:	Let them praise the name of the Lord,
	For his name alone is exalted;
Girls:	His splendor is above the earth and the heavens.
All:	(loudly) Praise the Lord.

Activity Sheet by Bev Gundersen © 1991 David C. Cook Publishing Co. Permission granted to reproduce for classroom use only.

Junior Electives

Service Projects For The Environment

In addition to the projects listed in these lessons your class or church can also serve in the following ways:

☑ 1. Become informed about ways you can help preserve the earth. Then spread the information you've learned to your families, church family, school, or neighborhood.

☑ 2. Develop recycling programs for aluminum, plastic, glass, and paper.

☑ 3. Start an "E-Team" club. To go along with the projects mentioned in the lessons you can place environmental slogans on buttons, banners, windsocks, visors, and T-shirts. Wear or use these items when working on the projects.

☑ 4. Collect and recycle paper bags for stores so more trees don't have to be cut down.

☑ 5. Learn to buy and spend wisely. Use products that don't pollute the environment.

☑ 6. "Adopt" an animal from a zoo or nature organization. They will provide information about your "pet" in return for donations to help feed and care for it.

☑ 7. Become involved in local tree-planting projects.

☑ 8. Go hunting for birds and animals on a nature "safari." See how many you can capture with your camera.

Junior Electives
Sports and Competition

It's How You Play the Game...

The issue of sports and competition is an important one for your Juniors. You may have already noticed how much they love to play competitive games. However, since they also have a high sensitivity to winning, the focus can easily shift from the game itself to the act of competition. When handled properly, competition can be the source of learning valuable lessons with application to many parts of life. However, when winning becomes the only goal, competition can become a hurtful experience.

In this unit, you will have the opportunity to help your kids discover many of the valuable life lessons to be learned from healthy competition, such as learning that it's OK to lose and how to lose gracefully; sometimes life isn't fair; and the benefits of working together as a team. You will also be able to point out the pitfalls of destructive competition, such as the temptation to win at any price and seeing the opposition as the enemy.

By taking your students to Scripture, you will also help them see how sports and competition can be an important arena in which to learn how their actions and attitudes can bring honor, or dishonor, to God.

Sports and Competition Overview

Unit Verse: Train yourself to be godly. For physical training is of some value, but godliness has value for all things, holding promise for both the present life and the life to come. I Timothy 4:7b-8.

Unit Affirmation: I CAN HONOR GOD BY THE WAY I PLAY!

LESSON	TITLE	OBJECTIVE	SCRIPTURE BASE
Lesson #1	God and My Bod	That your students will use their bodies and minds to glorify God who created them.	Judges 16:1-21
Lesson #2	Fair Play	That your students will honor God by treating competitors fairly.	Genesis 27:1-45; 29:15-28
Lesson #3	It's How You Play the Game	That your students will see that their attitudes about winning and losing are more important than the outcome of competition.	Genesis 41:41-44; 45:1-24
Lesson #4	Go Team, Go!	That your students will know that God's design for our lives includes working and playing together.	Philippians 2:1-5, 19-23

Partners

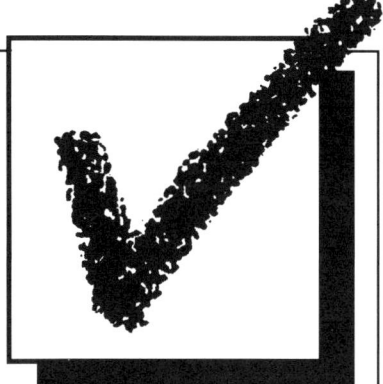

Keeping Parents Informed and Involved!

For the next few weeks your Junior-age child will be part of a group learning about Sports and Competition. *Partners* is a planned parent piece to keep you informed of what will be taught during this exciting series.

PREVIEW...

Sports and Competition

The whole area of sports and competition is very important to Junior-age children. Besides the fact that they naturally enjoy competitive activities, the emphasis on children's sports in our country has grown tremendously over the past ten or more years. Many Juniors have been in organized sports since they were quite young. This early involvement in highly competitive settings can have a positive or negative effect on kids. When handled properly, competition can be the source of valuable lessons with application to many parts of life. However, when winning becomes the primary goal, competition can become a hurtful experience for kids, teaching them as many negative lessons as positive ones.

During this unit, your kids will have a chance to take a look at both the positive and negative effects of competition. Through the use of the Unit Verse and Unit Affirmation, they will also see that being a Christian has a direct influence on how we respond to competitive settings.

Unit Verse:

Train yourself to be godly. For physical training is of some value, but godliness has value for all things, holding promise for both the present life and the life to come.
I Timothy 4:7b-8

Unit Affirmation:

I CAN HONOR GOD BY THE WAY I PLAY!

PRINCIPLES...

Sports and Competition

Healthy competition can be the source for learning many important life principles. During this unit, your kids will discuss the following:

PRINCIPLE #1:

IT'S OK TO LOSE. As simple as it sounds, this is an attitude toward life that many children never learn well. When kids participate in healthy competition, they learn that everyone loses sometimes and that losing or winning is not as important as playing well. However, when competition is out of balance, they learn that it's OK to do anything possible to win. Both of these attitudes carry over into other parts of life.

PRINCIPLE #2:

LIFE ISN'T ALWAYS FAIR. Junior-age kids have a high sensitivity to things being fair. In sports and competition, they will sometimes experience calls and judgments that are not fair. Sometimes authorities make mistakes or other things happen that may seem unfair at the time. In healthy competition, kids learn that they can choose how they will respond when things are not fair. They can accept the judgment and continue to enjoy the game, or they can let the seeming injustice spoil the rest of the game for them. Again, the application to other parts of life is clear.

PRINCIPLE #3:

TREAT EVERYONE WITH RESPECT. Good sportsman-

©1991 David C. Cook Publishing Co. Permission granted to reproduce for distribution to parents only.

Partners

ship is as much a part of healthy competition as good skills. Learning to treat all coaches, team members, and the other team with sincere respect is not always easy. In healthy competition, kids learn that their attitudes and actions toward the other team are a reflection on their own team. Seeing competitors as friends rather than enemies is an important skill with carryover to many areas of life.

PRINCIPLE #4:

TEAMWORK IS THE KEY TO WINNING. Perhaps the most valuable lesson kids learn in healthy competition is the benefit of teamwork. Because we live in a highly individualized culture, kids often grow up believing the philosophy of "every man for himself." But Scripture makes it clear that God never intended for any of us to live life alone. In fact, just the opposite is true. When we learn the skills of working with others, we find that we can accomplish much more than we could ever do on our own. We also maximize our own potential when we take the time to care for other team members and play off everyone's strengths and weaknesses. Teams that win are teams that know how to work together! The same is true of many settings in life. The value of learning to work together as a team is applicable to family life, school classes, and (someday!) the work environment.

PRINCIPLE #5:

WE CAN CHOOSE TO HONOR GOD THROUGH OUR ACTIONS AND ATTITUDES. As they study the Unit Verse and Unit Affirmation, the kids will discover that God has a lot to say about how we act in competitive settings. Choosing to treat others with respect and kindness is always honoring to God, and that includes during competition. Name-calling, harassing, and starting fights with the opposing team are all destructive, and not a part of healthy competition. As a higher value is placed on living the Christian life instead of on winning, they will once again learn a key life skill.

PRACTICE...

Sports and Competition

1. PLAY TOGETHER AS A FAMILY.

One of the best places for kids to learn the lessons of healthy competition is at home. Play together often, being aware of the life principles outlined above. Make your play times laboratories of learning how to compete well.

2. LEARN THE RULES OF GOOD SPORTSMANSHIP.

Make a poster of the following rules, discussing each one as a family. Post it where you can all see it and refer to it during family playtimes.

RULE #1:

IT'S OK TO LOSE. Learning that losing is OK removes the pressure to always be "on top" and frees us to enjoy the game!

RULE #2:

SEE COMPETITORS AS FRIENDS, NOT ENEMIES! Working hard to win is OK, as long as we don't get so caught up in the competition that we see the other team players as enemies. That's when we get into hurtful behavior.

RULE #3:

TREAT EVERYONE WITH COURTESY AND RESPECT. Name-calling, put-downs, booing, hissing and fighting are always inappropriate behavior, no matter what the setting!

RULE #4:

PLAYING IS MORE IMPORTANT THAN WINNING. Winning is nice. Having fun competing is better. Working hard to improve your own skills and having fun is best! Don't let the goal of winning be so important that it robs you of all the fun of playing the game!

3. OBSERVE YOUR CHILD IN COMPETITIVE SETTINGS.

If your child plays on an organized sports team, make a point to observe his or her behavior the next time there is a game. Look for attitudes and actions that will tell you his or her attitude toward competition. Having fun, learning new skills and treating others with respect are more important than winning!

Sports and Competition

Lesson 1

God and My Bod

Aim: That your students will use their bodies and minds to glorify God who created them

Scripture: Judges 16:1-21

Unit Verse: Train yourself to be godly. For physical training is of some value, but godliness has value for all things, holding promise for both the present life and the life to come. I Timothy 4:7b-8

Unit Affirmation: I CAN HONOR GOD BY THE WAY I PLAY!

✓ Planning Ahead

1. Photocopy Activity Sheets (pages 95 and 96)—one for each student.
2. Prepare the Unit Affirmation poster by writing across the top of a large poster board, I CAN HONOR GOD BY THE WAY I PLAY! Under the title, write the numbers 1-4 vertically down the left-hand side.
3. Prepare supplies for fingerpainting as described in LIVING THE LESSON.

1 Setting the Stage (5-10 minutes)

WHAT YOU'LL DO
- Play two games that use God's gifts of strong bodies and minds

WHAT YOU'LL NEED
- OPTIONAL: Two award ribbons or small prizes

2 Introducing the Issue (20 minutes)

WHAT YOU'LL DO
- Recognize the human body and mind as gifts from God
- Discover ways to develop (train) the body and mind
- Introduce the Unit Affirmation poster

WHAT YOU'LL NEED
- "Getting Stronger . . ." Activity Sheet (page 95)
- Unit Affirmation poster

3 Searching the Scriptures (20 minutes)

WHAT YOU'LL DO
- Read a letter showing accountability to God for the way bodies and minds are used
- Make book or Bible covers emphasizing the Unit Verse

WHAT YOU'LL NEED
- Bibles
- "Mr. Might-Have-Been" Activity Sheet (page 96)
- Large sheets of paper—one for each student, markers or crayons

4 Living the Lesson (5-10 minutes)

WHAT YOU'LL DO
- Make fingerpaint pictures to express ways they can use their bodies and minds wisely

WHAT YOU'LL NEED
- Black cherry, grape, or strawberry powdered gelatin, paper, water in a shallow container
- Paper towels, newspapers

Lesson 1

Sports and Competition

✓ Setting the Stage (5-10 minutes)

Begin your class today by involving kids in two games, one that uses brain power, and one that uses muscle power. As they arrive, instruct them to take a sheet of paper, write the word "RECREATION" across the top and then write down as many words as they can make using the letters in "Recreation," such as eat, create. They can only use the exact letters that are in the word, i.e., they can make a word with two "e's", but they cannot make a word with two "t's." When everyone has arrived and had a chance to make a list, let kids compare them. **Who made the most words?** Present an award ribbon or small prize to the one student who finds the most words. Next involve the kids in an arm-wrestling tournament. Pair them off for the first round. Then let the winners of the first round pair off and compete for round two. Continue in this way until you have one winner left. Present a small prize or a ribbon to this person.

Today we are starting a new unit on sports and competition, an area that most kids your age really enjoy. But sometimes it's hard to keep it all in proper perspective. How did you feel about not winning the arm-wrestling or finding the most words? What if you are the one with next to the most words, or no words at all? Does that mean you are a loser? What happens when playing and competing stop being fun and become hurtful? In the weeks ahead, we'll talk about how to make sports and competition an enjoyable—not stressful—part of our lives!

✓ Introducing the Issue (20 minutes)

Sports and competition fall into the category of play, or recreation. Playing games as a way to relax, reduce stress and have fun is as old as mankind. But playing games also serves another purpose, and that is to help us develop and make good use of two very important gifts God has given us—our bodies and our minds.

When we are born, God gives each of us a strong body and good mind. But what we do with them is up to us. It is our responsibility to take care of them, and learn how to use them wisely. We can learn a lot about how to do that from playing sports. For instance, supposing you want to play in Little League. When you sign up for the team the first time, are you going to go out there and be a terrific player? (No. No one automatically knows how to play any sport really well.) **What do you have to do to become a great ballplayer?** (Go through training, which means learning the basic skills from the coach and then practicing a lot!) **Training is the**

Sports and Competition

Lesson 1

key to being good at any sport!

Divide your kids into groups of three or four and tell them that they have just become coaches of a soccer or baseball team (or whatever sport your kids most enjoy). Today is the first day of training, and in a few minutes they will be meeting with their team. Their task is to write a coach's speech for this occasion, which will tell the team the expectations and rules for training, and motivate them to do a great job. Give them a few minutes to write, and then ask each group to read its speech to the rest of the class. As they do, begin a list on the board of the elements of training that are mentioned, such as discipline, and practice. When all the speeches are done, ask the class to think of other elements of training that could be added to your list. Your list should include: Attending practice, regular exercise, proper diet, working together as a team. **As you can see, training is hard work! But what are the benefits?** (Learning to be a good player and having a good team.) **The bottom line in training is *choices*. Coaches can teach us what to do, but we have to *choose* to do it! What would happen if I sleep instead of exercise, and never go to practice?** (I'd be a lousy ballplayer!)

Just as none of us are automatically good ball players, none of us automatically have strong bodies and minds. Distribute copies of the activity sheet "Getting Stronger . . . ." (page 95). **We can think of developing strong bodies and minds like being in training. What are some choices we can make to develop and make good use of our bodies?** Have kids write some ideas inside the weights on the "Body" side of the strong weightlifter's barbells. Possibilities: Turn off the TV and do something active, join a sport team, ride your bike, eat a healthy diet, swim, build something big (like a doghouse or a snow fort). **What are poor choices we can make that "break training" of our bodies?** Have kids write these ideas on the "Body" side of the weak weightlifter's barbells. Possibilities: Watch too much TV, eat too much junk food, use drugs or alcohol to have fun. **What are some choices we can make to develop and make good use of our minds?** Write these on the "Mind" side of the strong weightlifter's barbells. Ideas: read, work puzzles, play strategy games (like chess). **What are poor choices that "break training" of our minds?** Be alone too much, watch too much TV, read or watch "junk."

Finish the activity sheet by reinforcing the training tip at the bottom.

Display the Unit Affirmation poster (See PLANNING AHEAD.) and read the Affirmation aloud together. **Our bodies and minds are wonderful gifts from God that we can treasure all our lives. Using these gifts wisely is one way we can bring honor to God.** Write "making good choices about what to play" on the first line. **Now let's take a look at a Bible story that illustrates**

Lesson 1

Sports and Competition

someone who *didn't* make good choices about the use of his body and mind!

✓ Searching the Scriptures (20 minutes)

What should be our attitude about using the bodies and minds God has given us? Let students talk about this briefly. **Do you think we have any obligations to God about how we use them?**

We can get some answers to these questions by looking at the life of one Bible person who could be nicknamed "Mr. Might-Have-Been." Have students turn to the book of Judges in the Bible. Distribute copies of the activity sheet "Mr. Might-Have-Been" (page 96). Ask someone to read the directions. Kids can work on this exercise individually. When they have finished, students can take turns reading the letter aloud with the answers. Answers are: Samson, Philistines, lion, riddles, revenge, I or Samson, Delilah, eleven hundred, overpower or tie up or subdue, nagging or prodding, shave, Lord, prison.

What kind of a body and mind did God give Samson? (He was extra-strong and smart.) **Why did God give him these gifts?** (He was to use them to deliver the Israelites from their enemies.) **Why did Samson wear his hair long?** Explain that Samson was a Nazirite. They were people who were set apart for special service to God. Samson's long hair was an outward sign of an inward promise to serve God faithfully all his life. Besides not cutting their hair, Nazirites were also not to drink alcoholic beverages. **How did Samson use his strength and mind?** (Wasted them on foolish things for personal pleasure and revenge.) **How should he have used them?** (To help others, deliver the Israelites from their enemies, to tell the Philistines about God.) Because the Philistines admired physical strength, Samson had a natural opening to share with them the truth about God. Instead, he chose to use God's gifts for personal satisfaction.

Once Samson had to escape from Gaza in the middle of the night. He pulled up the doors and posts of the city wall and carried them toward Hebron. Those gates weighed thousands of pounds and yet he carried them thirty-eight miles away!

How did he begin to feel about his miraculous deeds? (Proud, bragged that he had done them himself.) **Are we ever tempted to forget about who enables us to do the things we do? If so, when?** Encourage students to share some times when this has been a problem for them. Sharing some event from your own life may help them identify with you.

Sports and Competition

Lesson 1

What kind of lifestyle did Samson have? (He became friends with the enemies of God and God's people.) **Why do you think Samson was deceived by Delilah?** Point out that he wanted to be with her more than he wanted to see the truth. He chose to misuse his mind by believing lies and yielding to her temptations. **Do we ever choose to ignore the truth and give in to temptations? If so, when?** Help students see that whenever we let someone talk us into doing wrong things such as disobeying parents, taking drugs, shoplifting, or cheating we are ignoring the truth and yielding to temptations.

What happened when Samson's hair was cut off? (He was helpless against his enemies.) Help kids see that Samson's hair was not really the source of his strength. The true source of his strength was God. The long hair was part of his promise to serve God, but before it was cut Samson had already broken his vows. His lifestyle was the opposite of a Nazirite. Perhaps the saddest commentary on his life is that "He did not know that the Lord had left him" (verse 20).

What happened to Samson after his hair was cut? (His enemies captured him, blinded him, made him a slave; forced him to grind grain in a prison.) **Why do you think God allowed this to happen?** (He wanted him to realize the consequences of his disobedient choices.) Point out that when we live in disobedience to His will for us God doesn't step in and make everything all right again. Because He has given us the freedom of choice we also have the freedom to ruin our lives. People who abuse their bodies by bad health habits or by using drugs pay the consequences of broken health. Those who use their minds to plan crimes end up in prison.

Ask students to turn to the Unit Verse, I Timothy 4:7b-8, and read it together. **Samson was strong physically. What do you think his godly muscles were like?** (Weak and flabby.) **How can we build up "godly" muscles?** (By praying, reading the Bible, trying to find God's will for us, obeying God's laws.) **Was Samson's physical strength of value to him in prison? Why or why not?** (No. He could only use it to grind grain, to serve his enemies.)

God gave Samson another chance to train himself to be godly. Samson asked forgiveness for his sin and God enabled him to fulfil the purpose for which he had been born. Have someone read aloud Hebrews 11:32-34. **Samson was victorious over his enemies not by his strength, but by his faith in God. There may be times when physical strength fails, but godly strength helps us now and forever.**

Distribute the large sheets of paper and drawing materials. Kids will fold the paper to make book covers for their Bibles.

Lesson 1

Sports and Competition

Each week during this unit they will add a sentence emphasizing a truth from the Unit Verse. Write this open-ended sentence on the board and have students copy it and write an ending that is meaningful to them: We can train ourselves to be godly by . . . If you have time, kids can illustrate the sentence. Keep the covers in the classroom for use throughout the unit.

✓ Living the Lesson (5-10 minutes)

What are some ways we can use our bodies and minds wisely? Help kids see that whenever we use our bodies and minds to the best of our ability and in ways that are in accordance with God's plans we are using them wisely. Examples of some ways we can use our bodies and minds wisely are: practicing good health habits such as getting needed sleep, eating nutritious meals, and getting regular exercise; playing sports; studying at school; reading and learning more of God's Word.

Paul Anderson, an out-spoken Christian weightlifter, held the record and title of "World's Strongest Man" for many years. He once lifted over six-thousand pounds in a back lift, yet said that he couldn't get through a minute of the day without Jesus Christ. Every day he read the Bible and spent time in prayer. He trained himself in godliness as well as physical ways.

Before class, cut 9" x 12" pieces of nonporous paper—one for each student. Use butcher or shelf paper, or commercial fingerpainting paper. Fill a shallow container, such as a 9" x 13" casserole dish, with water and have one three-ounce container of gelatin for every four to six students.

When we use our hands we combine our body and mind to cooperate in achieving a goal. Explain that students will use their hands to make fingerpaintings to show ways they can use their body and mind for God. Dip the papers into water and then scatter one or two teaspoons of powdered gelatin over the wet paper. Kids can write or paint pictures of ways to use their minds and bodies for God. The gelatin is fun to work with because the texture changes from grainy to slippery, to sticky, to grainy again when dry. It also smells good! Allow paintings to dry before students take them home or display them.

Invite volunteers to pray and thank God for their minds and bodies.

Getting Stronger... ✓

TRAINING TIP:

The Choice is YOURS! God gave each of us strong bodies and sound minds. But keeping them strong and using them wisely is up to us!

Activity Sheet by Linda Kondracki © 1991 David C. Cook Publishing Co. Permission granted to reproduce for classroom use only.

✓ Mr. Might-Have-Been

Fill in the blanks with words found in the references shown in the parentheses. All passages are from the book of Judges.

Dear Ezra,

I'm writing to tell you about our friend, _____ (13:24). As you know, God gave him great strength because He wanted Samson to deliver us from our enemies, the _____ (13:5). Remember how he tore a _____ (14:6) apart with his bare hands? His long hair was a symbol to everyone of his promise to follow God.

Samson was smart too, but he wasted his mind making up _____ (14:12) and thinking up ways to get _____ (15:7) on his personal enemies when he should have been seeking God and leading our nation to victory.

He began to brag about his deeds, saying "_____ (15:16) did these things." It was sad to see he had forgotten who gave him his body and mind. You said he could get in trouble unless he realized he was answerable to God for these gifts. How right you were!

After you moved away, Samson got involved with the very enemies he was supposed to defeat. He broke his promise to God.

I'm sorry to tell you that Samson fell in love with one of these Philistine women. Her name was _____ (16:4). Their rulers each agreed to pay her _____ (16:5) shekels of silver if she could find out the secret of his strength so they could _____ (16:5) him.

How foolish he was! She kept _____ (16:16) him to tell her. Even though he knew she lied to him, he wanted to believe her. At last he told her that the secret was his long hair. She hid men in her room and called one of them to _____ (16:19) off Samson's hair while he was asleep. When he woke up he thought he could use his strength to save him from his enemies. He didn't even realize that the _____ (16:20) had left him! God let him face the consequences of his choices.

Now our friend is a blind slave grinding grain in the _____ (16:21) of Gaza. If he had remembered and thanked God for the gifts of his body and mind and used them for Him, this wouldn't have happened. Perhaps he will still turn to the Lord before it is too late. Please pray for him.

　　Sadly,
　　Joel

Activity Sheet by Bev Gundersen © 1991 David C. Cook Publishing Co. Permission granted to reproduce for classroom use only.

Sports and Competition

Lesson 2

Fair Play

Aim: That your students will honor God by treating competitors fairly

Scripture: Genesis 27:1-45; 29:15-28

Unit Verse: Train yourself to be godly. For physical training is of some value, but godliness has value for all things, holding promise for both the present life and the life to come. I Timothy 4:7b-8

Unit Affirmation: I CAN HONOR GOD BY THE WAY I PLAY!

✓ Planning Ahead

1. Photocopy activity sheets (pages 103 and 104)—one for each student.
2. Prepare questions as described in SETTING THE STAGE.

1 Setting the Stage (5-10 minutes)

WHAT YOU'LL DO
- Play a game to simulate an example of cheating

WHAT YOU'LL NEED
- Seven questions, one answer card
- OPTIONAL: Small prizes or treats for everyone in the class

2 Introducing the Issue (20 minutes)

WHAT YOU'LL DO
- Compare and contrast the differences between being fair and cheating
- Participate in a creative activity to illustrate the difference between fair play and cheating
- Add a phrase to the Unit Affirmation poster

WHAT YOU'LL NEED
- "Fair Play!" Activity Sheet (page 103)
- Something to use as a microphone, such as a tablespoon
- Unit Affirmation poster

3 Searching the Scriptures (20 minutes)

WHAT YOU'LL DO
- Discover how cheating can come back to haunt us

WHAT YOU'LL NEED
- Bibles
- "Cheaters Never Win" Activity Sheets (page 104)
- Bible covers from Lesson One, drawing materials

4 Living the Lesson (5-10 minutes)

WHAT YOU'LL DO
- Practice ways to can compete fairly by playing a game

WHAT YOU'LL NEED
- Two or more inflated balloons, stopwatch or clock with second hand

97

Lesson 2

Sports and Competition

✓ Setting the Stage (5-10 minutes)

To open your class today, involve the kids in a simulation of cheating. Before class, write seven very difficult review questions or Bible trivia questions. Write the answers on a 3" x 5" card. As your students arrive, divide them into two teams and tell them you are going to play a review game. Quietly give the card of answers to a player on one of the teams and tell him or her to share these with the other team players. Play the game by alternating questions between teams, and keeping track of points for correct answers. Before the game is over, the cheating will probably be pointed out. **Why isn't it fair for me to give the answers to one of the teams?** (It's cheating.) **Cheating is an important topic for us to talk about during this unit on sports and competition, and that's just what we are going to do today!**

✓ Introducing the Issue (20 minutes)

How did it feel to be on the winning team and know you were cheating or had teammates who were cheating? Allow for responses. **How did it feel to be on the losing team and when you knew you had not been treated fairly?** Allow for responses. **What else were any of you (winners and losers) feeling during our little simulation?** Allow for responses. **What is cheating? Why do you think people cheat?** (They don't want to lose, they will do anything to get what they want) **No one likes to lose. But the important thing we need to learn as we grow up is that everyone loses sometimes! You cannot win all the time. In fact, learning how to lose is an important part of playing games.**

Write the following headings on your board: FAIR PLAY and CHEATING. Ask kids to brainstorm the differences between the two. As they mention things, write them on the board. When you are finished, your list should look similar to this:

FAIR PLAY
1. More fun for everyone
2. Respectful of all players
3. Others will want to play with me
4. I will lose sometimes
5. Honors God

CHEATING
1. Takes away fun for everyone
2. Disrespectful of others, hurts others
3. Others may be angry with me and may stop playing with me
4. I may win more often, but I will still lose sometimes
5. Dishonors God

Sports and Competition

Lesson 2

Distribute copies of the activity sheet "Fair Play!" (page 103), and briefly discuss each box together. **What do you think is happening in the first box?** (The child who is being accused of cheating may have moved too many spaces on the board, or the accuser may be trying to control the game by accusations of cheating when it wasn't happening.) **What do you think is happening in the second box?** (The ball has actually touched the ground, but the child is going to try to say it didn't.) **What do you think is happening in the third box?** (This box shows one of the possible results of cheating, others don't want to play with you.) **What do you think is happening in the last box?** (Our cheating can influence what others think about what it means to be a Christian.)

Divide the class into four groups and assign one of the scenarios to each group. Their task will be to fill in the boxes to the right and left of their scenario, showing ways the child in the scenario could respond fairly or cheating. Then let them choose *one* of the following ways to present their illustrations to the rest of the class:

1) Drama. The group can plan and act out both of the illustrations.

2) Art. The group can make a series of pictures to present the illustrations. These can take the form of a cartoon strip, a picture gallery, or a story-book.

3) Journalism. The group can present its illustrations in the form of a news report. This could be an evening news show or a news flash bulletin. It could also be a "man-on-the-street" type interview. Have available something that can be used as a microphone for this group to use.

When they are finished, give each group a few minutes to share its work with the rest of the class.

Display the Unit Affirmation poster and read the affirmation aloud together. Ask the kids to think of a phrase they can add to the next line. Possibilities might include: "when I treat others fairly," or simply, "by playing fair." **God's word is very clear about cheating being wrong. Perhaps the biggest reason it is wrong is because it can only be hurtful to others and ourselves. Let's look at someone in the Bible who learned that lesson about cheating the hard way!**

✓ Searching the Scriptures (20 minutes)

Do you think cheating pays off? Allow students to briefly discuss this. **Let's see what happened to a cheater in Bible times.** Distribute copies of the activity sheet "Cheaters Never Win" (page 104). You will read the story and students can follow along on their sheets. When you come to phrases in

Lesson 2

Sports and Competition

parentheses, let the kids respond with feeling!

Ask students to turn to Genesis 27:1-45. **Who thought up the scheme to cheat Esau?** (Rebekah, his mother.) **The family rivalry was fierce. Esau was his father's favorite and Jacob was his mother's favorite. If Rebekah thought up the scheme, was Jacob guilty of cheating? Why or why not?** (Yes. Jacob was equally guilty because he agreed to carry it out.)

How did she disguise Jacob so Isaac would think he was Esau? (Covered his hands, arms, and neck with goatskins.) Point out that not only were they deceiving Isaac, but they were also taking advantage of his disability of blindness.

Have someone read verses 11-13. **What was Jacob worried about the most?** (Getting caught.) **This bothered him more than the wrongness of the deed. What did Rebekah say about this?** (To let any blame fall on her.) Jacob and Esau were twins. God had promised from their birth that Jacob would be the leader of the family, but Rebekah decided to help God out by taking a deceitful shortcut.

Do you think that we should help achieve our goals by cheating? Why or why not? Let students discuss this briefly. Focus on questions such as: **Is it all right to take steroids in order to excel in sports? If you studied for a test but forgot an answer, should you look at a classmate's paper? What if your friend needs to pass a test and asks you to move a little so she or he can see your paper? What can happen if we take steroids for sports? What happens if you cheat on a test or allow a friend to cheat? When is it easy not to cheat? When is it hard not to cheat?**

Ask students to check out verses 19, 20, and 24. **What did Jacob do?** (Lied.) **One sin leads to another. In order to carry out his deceit Jacob lied three times. How do you think Jacob felt about lying about God?** (Guilty, separated from God, uncomfortable, miserable.) **How did Esau feel when he found out Jacob had cheated him?** (Sad, bitter, furious, wanted to kill his brother.) **How do you feel when people cheat you?** Briefly let students share their feelings and experiences.

What did Jacob have to do because he had cheated his brother? (Leave home.) **How do you think this made him feel?** (Sad, lonely, sorry he had tricked Esau.) Cheaters usually get punished sooner or later. Rebekah also paid for her trickery by never seeing her favorite son again after he fled from Esau.

Have students turn to Genesis 29:26 and read it aloud. **Why do you think Laban didn't tell Jacob about this custom?** Laban must have known that Jacob would be reluctant to wait until Leah was married so he could marry Rachel. By not telling him about the custom, Laban tricked Jacob into working seven years for him free. **In the paraphrase how did Jacob feel about**

Sports and Competition

Lesson 2

this trick? (Furious.) The tables had turned and now the deceiver was deceived. When someone treats us as badly as we have treated them we are angry and hurt. Jacob's cheating had backfired on him.

What did Jacob do after he learned the truth? (Worked seven more years so he could marry Rachel.) Jacob realized that taking shortcuts to reach a goal doesn't work. The results are usually not what we expected or wanted. Jacob learned from these experiences and chose to have a personal relationship with God.

Through his struggles he learned how to patiently obey and follow the Lord so that God later changed his name from Jacob (deceiver/cheater) to Israel (he shall be prince of God).

What do you think we can learn from Jacob's experiences? (Cheating never pays for anyone.) Even if we don't get caught, the personal damage done to our relationship with God and other people is too costly a price to pay for temporary benefits.

Have students repeat the Unit Verse, I Timothy 4:7b-8, while they walk in place. **How can we train ourselves in godliness by the treatment we give competitors?** (Fair treatment of others honors God and helps us grow spiritually and morally.) **What promise does this method bring in the present life?** (When we treat others fairly, they also treat us fairly.) **What value does it have in the life to come?** Help students see that the everlasting value of treating competitors fairly is that it prepares us to live with God who treats all people fairly.

Distribute the Bible covers the kids worked on in Lesson One. Write this open-ended sentence on the board and have students complete it as they wish: Fair treatment of our competitors has value because . . . If time allows, kids can draw pictures to illustrate their completed statements.

✓ Living the Lesson (5-10 minutes)

There's no better way to learn to treat competitors fairly than by playing a game. For this game you will need a fairly large space. Because it is an active group game it can also get noisy so plan accordingly.

Balloon Blast: Divide your class into two teams. One team becomes Blasters and the other Backers. Appoint a timekeeper and then toss up a balloon between the two teams. The Backers try to protect the balloon by batting it out of reach while the Blasters try to break it by grabbing it, slapping it between their hands or stepping on it. Write down the time it takes the Blasters to break the balloon. Reverse the play by having the Blasters become the Backers.

Lesson 2

Sports and Competition

Again record the time it takes to break the balloon. The team with the shortest time wins.

Have everyone sit down as a group. Discuss the competition briefly by focusing on these questions: **As you played this game how did you feel about your opponents? As the game got more active did you find yourself getting more physically aggressive about stopping your competitors? Was winning more important than how you treated others?**

Have someone look up and read aloud Luke 6:31. **How did Jesus say we needed to treat others?** (As we would want to be treated.) **This Golden Rule applies to all competition and is the key to living a life that is honoring to God.**

Close in prayer, asking God's help to honor Him by treating our competitors fairly.

Fair Play! ✓

	"You cheated!"	
	"No one saw that..." BOUNCE!	
	"You're a cheater! Go find someone else to play with!" MARBLES	
	"He's the biggest cheat on the team!" "Yeah, and he's the one who keeps talking about being a Christian!" WAP!	

Activity Sheet by Linda Kondracki © 1991 David C. Cook Publishing Co. Permission granted to reproduce for classroom use only.

Cheaters Never Win

When Isaac was old and nearly blind, he called his older son, Esau, to him and asked him to go hunting and prepare a tasty meal for him. (YUM YUM.) "It may be the last meal I'll eat before I die so I will give you the eldest son blessing when you return," Isaac said.

Now Jacob was Isaac's younger son. His mother, Rebekah, and he planned to cheat Esau so Isaac would give Jacob the blessing instead. It was an elaborate scheme and required perfect timing. Jacob was very nervous but he wanted the blessing so badly he would do anything to get it. (OH, OH!) The hoax worked perfectly. Jacob pretended to be Esau, got his father's blessing and escaped before Esau was back from hunting.

However, cheaters never really win and Jacob was about to find that out the hard way. (OH, OH!) Esau was furious when he discovered how Jacob had cheated him. Jacob had to run away to his distant relatives to escape Esau's death threat. (DA DA DUM, DA DA DUM, DA DA DUM DUM DUM)

While he was there Jacob went to work as a shepherd for his uncle Laban. He fell in love with Laban's beautiful daughter Rachel. (WOW!) He agreed to work seven years to get her as his wife. At the end of that time Jacob was married to Laban's daughter. A heavy veil hid her face and it was not until the day after the wedding that Jacob discovered his new wife was not the lovely Rachel (WOW!), but was her plain sister, Leah, instead! (OH, OH!) Now it was Jacob's turn to be furious.

He stormed over to Laban's tent (STOMP! STOMP! STOMP!) and demanded an explanation. Laban insisted that the custom of that country was that the older daughter had to be married before the younger one. He promised to give Rachel (WOW!) to Jacob if he would work seven years more for him. Although he ground his teeth and shook his fist in anger, there was nothing Jacob could do. He loved Rachel (WOW!) so much that he would do anything to get her. A sadder (SNIFF, SNIFF) but wiser young man wearily agreed to work another seven years for his beautiful bride.

As he returned to the sheep (DA DA DUM, DA DA DUM, DA DA DUM DUM DUM), one could almost have heard Jacob mutter, "I've learned my lesson. Cheaters never win. From now on I'll do to others as I would have them do to me." (HOORAY!)

Activity Sheet by Bev Gundersen © 1991 David C. Cook Publishing Co. Permission granted to reproduce for classroom use only.

Sports and Competition

Lesson 3

It's How You Play the Game

Aim: That your students will see that their attitudes about winning and losing are more important than the outcome of competition
Scripture: Genesis 41:41-44, 45:1-24
Unit Verse: Train yourself to be godly. For physical training is of some value, but godliness has value for all things, holding promise for both the present life and the life to come. I Timothy 4:7b-8

Unit Affirmation: CAN HONOR GOD BY THE WAY I PLAY!

✓ Planning Ahead

1. Photocopy Activity Sheets (pages 111 and 112)—one for each student.
2. Prepare 45 letter cards (approximately 6" x 6") to spell out the phrase: "It's not whether you win or lose, but how you play the game." Write only one letter on each card.
3. Prepare two roleplay cards as described in LIVING THE LESSON.

1 Setting the Stage (5-10 minutes)
WHAT YOU'LL DO
- Play a game to discover the theme for this lesson

WHAT YOU'LL NEED
- Letter cards

2 Introducing the Issue (20 minutes)
WHAT YOU'LL DO
- Talk about attitudes and behavior of good winners and losers
- Make a "Competitor's Handbook"
- OPTIONAL: Play a game to reinforce being a "good sport"
- Add a phrase to the Unit Affirmation poster

WHAT YOU'LL NEED
- "Competitor's Handbook" Activity Sheet (page 111)
- OPTIONAL: A ping-pong ball
- Unit Affirmation poster

3 Searching the Scriptures (20 minutes)
WHAT YOU'LL DO
- See how a wealthy, important, godly man chose not to gloat over his poor, obscure brothers

WHAT YOU'LL NEED
- Bibles
- "The Winner and Still Champion" Activity Sheet (page 112)
- Bible covers from Lesson Two, drawing materials

4 Living the Lesson (5-10 minutes)
WHAT YOU'LL DO
- Dramatize good attitudes and behavior for competition

WHAT YOU'LL NEED
- Roleplay cards

Lesson 3

Sports and Competition

✓ Setting the Stage (5-10 minutes)

Before class, pin the 45 letter cards (See PLANNING AHEAD.) to a bulletin board or attach them to the wall in the correct order, but with the letters facing the wall so they cannot be seen. To play this game, let kids take turns guessing a letter of the alphabet. If the letter is on one of the cards, turn that letter card(s) over so it can be read. Continue letting students take turns guessing letters until someone guesses the phrase correctly. **What does this phrase mean?** (Allow for responses) **Looking at this phrase, what do you think our lesson is about today?** (Good sportsmanship.) **Competition can be a good thing. It can keep us motivated to keep working hard to learn new skills and to do our best in the game itself. But if we are not careful, it can work against us by making winning more important than learning new skills and just enjoying the process of competing! Today we want to talk about how we can keep that from happening.**

✓ Introducing the Issue (20 minutes)

What does it mean to be a "good sport?" Allow for responses. **What does it mean to be a "poor sport?"** Allow for responses. **What are some examples of being a "poor sport"?** (Booing and hissing at the other team, gloating over winning, throwing a temper tantrum over losing.) **What are the results of being a "poor sport"?** Help your kids see that, just like cheating, being a poor sport is hurtful to others and ourselves. **When we compete, it is important to remember Luke 6:31. The secret to being a good competitor is to treat the competition the way we want to be treated.**

Distribute copies of the activity sheet "Competitor's Handbook" (page 111). Have kids cut the pages apart and staple them into a booklet and decorate the cover. Then work on the inside pages together. **What are some rules we could make that would help us be good sports?** Let kids share ideas, perhaps listing all their thoughts on the board. Then, present the following information as kids write these rules in their booklets:

1) IT'S OK TO LOSE. One of the biggest reasons we act inappropriately in competition is that we don't like to lose. Learning that losing is OK removes the pressure to always be "on top."

2) SEE COMPETITORS AS FRIENDS, NOT ENEMIES! Working hard to win is OK, as long as we don't get so caught up in the competition that we see the other team players as enemies. That's when we get into hurtful behavior. It helps to remember that the other side is made up of friends.

Sports and Competition

Lesson 3

3) TREAT ALL PEOPLE INVOLVED WITH COURTESY AND RESPECT. Coaches, teachers, and players are all people who deserve to be treated fairly and with respect. Name-calling, put-downs, booing, hissing, and fighting are always inappropriate behavior, no matter what the setting! There is a saying that says, "What goes around, comes around." Applied to this setting, it means that if we are disrespectful and hurtful to others, they will be disrespectful and hurtful to us. (Sounds a lot like something Jesus said, doesn't it?)

4) PLAYING IS MORE IMPORTANT THAN WINNING. Winning is nice. Having fun competing is better. Working hard to improve your own skills and having fun is best! Don't let the goal of winning be so important that it robs you of all the best parts of competition!

Now look at the next page in the Competitor's Handbook. This is an individual goal-setting exercise to help you think about your own level of sportsmanship. The first goal asks you to think of something you could improve to be a better competitor. Ask volunteers to share things they want to write here. Examples: I will speak kindly to members of the other team, or I will not get upset and say angry things when I lose. **The second goal helps you focus on you and think of a competition skill you could work hard to improve.** Examples: I will work hard to throw a good curve ball or I will improve my chess game by joining the chess club at school. **The last goal asks you to think of ways you can bring honor to God by the way you handle competition.** Examples here might be to congratulate other team members when they win, to tell competitors when I think they have done a good job, or by never saying anything disrespectful or hurtful before, during, or after competition. Conclude this discussion by reading the last page, Luke 6:31, together.

OPTIONAL: Give your students a chance to practice the rules of good sportsmanship by playing a game. If you have enough time and an appropriate space and weather, you might go outside and play an active game of their choosing. If not, stay around your table and play ping-pong ball soccer. Divide into two teams and have each team spread out around one half of the table. Place a ping-pong ball in the middle of the table. To play, each team tries to blow the ball over the edge of the other team's half of the table. As they play, observe examples of good or poor sportsmanship. After the game, take some time to discuss feelings and observations.

Display the Unit Affirmation poster and read the Affirmation aloud together. Ask kids to think of a phrase to add to the third line. Possibilities might be, "when I treat everyone with respect," or simply "by being a good sport."

Lesson 3

Sports and Competition

Sometimes it's easier to talk about being a good sport than it is to be one! Let's take a look at someone in the Bible who understood what it means to live out all the qualities of good sportsmanship!

✓ Searching the Scriptures (20 minutes)

Joseph was seventeen years old when his jealous brothers sold him into slavery. Thirteen years later he was extremely wealthy and had an important job which gave him great honors. Let's see what his attitude was toward his brothers when he met them again. Distribute copies of the activity sheet "The Winner and Still Champion" (page 112). Although this is written as a monologue you can have students take turns reading it if you desire.

Then have kids take turns reading Genesis 41:41-44. **How important was Joseph?** (Second in command of all Egypt.) **The king of Egypt called for Joseph to explain a dream that troubled him.** Ask someone to read verse 16. **What did Joseph say about his ability?** (He couldn't interpret dreams by himself, but God would help him.) This attitude of dependence on God was the trademark of Joseph's life. He knew that whether he was a slave, a prisoner, or in charge of all Egypt, God had made him in His likeness and loved him. This knowledge gave him a good self-image. It also allowed him to see others as worthwhile individuals regardless of how well they did things.

Ask someone to read Genesis 45:3. **Why do you think Joseph's brothers were afraid of him?** (Because they thought he would seek revenge on them.) Read verses 5-8. **How did Joseph feel about what had happened to him?** (It was all part of God's plan to save his family.) Point out that Joseph didn't look upon his brothers as the enemy. He didn't keep track of their losses and his gains.

Ask someone to read verse 8 aloud. **How did Joseph feel about all the honors he had been given?** (God had given all of them to him.) Point out that his attitude was not one of pride or boasting in personal accomplishments. **Why do you think people have a tendency to brag about winning?** (They think they did it, not God; they have to be better than others to feel they are worthwhile.)

Have students look at verses 9-11. **What was Joseph most concerned about?** (Seeing his family again and helping them.) The problem with competition is that there is always a loser. If you win, others may feel worthless. If you lose, you may feel worthless. Somebody may end up getting hurt. Joseph put a stop to this pain by his attitude. He chose not to base self-worth—his own or anyone else's—on winning or losing.

Sports and Competition

Lesson 3

Let students discuss their feelings about competition. Focus on questions such as: **Do you compete for fun or is winning the only reason? How do you feel when you win? When you play a game does your competition become your enemy? How do you feel when you lose at something? Is winning so important that you feel you're worthless if you lose?** Share something about your own attitudes. Being honest about yourself, including flaws, helps students identify with you and opens doors for personal relationships which Junior-age kids need with mature Christian adults.

What are some ways we can stop the hurt of competition? Talk about specific ways such as: sharing attention with other competitors, not keeping track of winning or losing, competing for fun, competing against yourself, pointing out how everyone had a part, letting your goal be how much you get out of it and not how good or bad people did. **A good thought to apply to situations is "If Jesus were my coach/teacher/parent, what would He say when I lose? What about when I win?"** Stress that self-worth is based on how God sees us, not on what we do. God sees us as His precious creations and the objects of His love.

Read Genesis 45:22. **What did Joseph do differently for Benjamin than he did for the other brothers?** (Gave him five times as many clothes plus a large sum of money.) Explain that Joseph and Benjamin were full brothers, born of the same mother, Rachel. All the other brothers were Joseph's half-brothers. When Joseph had been a boy, his brothers were very jealous of the preferential treatment their father gave him. Their fierce competition with him had brought about their plan to sell him as a slave. Since Joseph's disappearance Jacob had treated Benjamin as his favorite son.

In the drama, what did Joseph think about his brothers' attitude towards Benjamin? (That God had worked in their lives to change their attitudes about competition.) Ask someone to read Genesis 45:24 aloud. **Why do you think Joseph said this to his brothers?** Joseph had seen real evidence of his brothers' changed attitude about family competition. By giving Benjamin special gifts, perhaps he wanted to test them one more time to assure himself that their change was a permanent one.

What do you think would have happened if Joseph and his brothers continued competing against each other? (Joseph might have chosen to imprison or kill his brothers, Joseph might have demanded that his brothers bow down and serve him, it is unlikely that there would have been forgiveness and peace in the family, God's plan to take care of the Jewish people might have been hindered.)

What happens when Christians compete against each other? (God's plans may be hindered, God is dishonored, God's enemies are happy.) Ask

Lesson 3

Sports and Competition

someone to read Romans 15:5-7. **This is God's desire for His children. When we cooperate, we honor the Lord.**

Have students repeat the Unit Verse, I Timothy 4:7b-8, together while they jog in place. **How can we train ourselves to be godly while competing against others?** (By remembering that self-worth is based on who we are not what we do, considering competitors friends not enemies, doing our best and not trying to be the best.)

Distribute the Bible covers from Lesson one. Write this statement on the board and let the kids copy and complete it on their covers. I can train myself to be godly when my attitude toward competition is . . .

✓ Living the Lesson (5-10 minutes)

Before class, prepare two roleplay cards by writing these situations on index cards:

1. Tyson worked hard to make the team. He went to all the practices and was good. Everyone thought he would make it. When the players were listed, Tyson lost out to Nick who just transferred from another school. Nick hasn't played with the team, but he was the star-player for his former school.

2. Ever since first grade, Heather's mom has said, "Why can't you be like your sister, Erica? She always gets good grades." Now Heather found Erica crying in her bedroom because she got caught skipping class.

Hand out the cards and have volunteers roleplay the parts of Tyson, Nick, Heather, and Erica. Discuss the roleplays focusing on questions such as: **What kind of attitude do you think the characters in this situation showed? Why did they act or react that way? What could she or he have done differently?**

Have students think of situations where they need to have different attitudes about competition. Have silent prayer asking God to help change bad attitudes to good ones. Close with a praise prayer to God for His constant love which makes each person worthwhile.

Competitor's Handbook

The Competitor's Handbook

Rules of Good Sportsmanship

1._____

2._____

3._____

4._____

Personal Goals

1) One way I can improve my attitude and actions during competition is _____

2) A skill for competing I would like to learn or improve is _____

3) One way I can honor God when I compete is _____

The Golden Rule of Good Sportsmanship

Jesus set the standard for good sportsmanship when He said:
"Do to others as you would have them do to you." Luke 6:31

Activity Sheet by Linda Kondracki © 1991 David C. Cook Publishing Co. Permission granted to reproduce for classroom use only.

The Winner and Still Champion

Joseph: I can't believe I'm actually seeing my brothers after all these years—here in the palace, eating a meal in the same room with me! Who would have dreamed things would turn out this way?

Whenever I think of how they looked that day when they sold me as a slave, it sends chills down my spine. I thought I had lost everything—my home, my family, maybe my life. I spent thirteen years as a slave because of them. God was always with me. With Him I was a winner even when everyone else labeled me a loser. The day the king called me to help him was the beginning of great things for me. I can still scarcely believe that I am now one of the most important men in all Egypt! I wear fancy clothes and gold jewelry, ride in a royal chariot, and people bow down wherever I go. It seems to be too good to be true.

Now here are my brothers at my mercy. I wonder if they remember how I used to talk about my dreams picturing them bowing down to me? I could make them do that now. I could say "I told you so!" I could force them to be my slaves, toss them in prison, or put them to death as spies. That's what some people would do, but I don't want to do that. I've stopped competing with my brothers.

Dear God, I've missed them. I've tested them and know that they have really changed. Why Judah, who suggested selling me then, just offered to be my slave if I would let Benjamin return to our father. That has to be because You have been working in my brothers' lives as You have in mine. You planned it all, didn't You, God?

Just look at me, crying so loud everyone can hear me because I suddenly know how much I love my brothers. I love them and forgive them. I can't wait any longer . . .

(calling) Judah, Reuben, Benjamin, it's me, Joseph. Come close to me, all of you. Yes, I really am your brother, Joseph. Don't be worried. I forgive you. It's all right. God had it all planned out. Stop crying, you're getting my robe all wet. What do you mean you're losers? Don't you understand? When God is with you, you are winners. It's all in your attitude!

Activity Sheet by Bev Gundersen © 1991 David C. Cook Publishing Co. Permission granted to reproduce for classroom use only.

Sports and Competition

Lesson 4 ✓

Go Team, Go!

Aim: That your students will know that God's design for our lives includes working and playing together

Scripture: Philippians 2:1-5, 19-23

Unit Verse: Train yourself to be godly. For physical training is of some value, but godliness has value for all things, holding promise for both the present life and the life to come. I Timothy 4:7b-8

Unit Affirmation: I CAN HONOR GOD BY THE WAY I PLAY!

✓ Planning Ahead

1. Photocopy Activity Sheets (pages 119 and 120)—one for each student.
2. Make seven "character" signs by printing each of the following words in large letters on 8 1/2" x 11" or larger pieces of paper. Punch holes in the top edges and attach pieces of yarn long enough so students can wear the signs around their necks. Words: Right foot, left foot, leg, arm, hand, heart, stomach.

1 Setting the Stage (5-10 minutes)

WHAT YOU'LL DO

- Work on jigsaw puzzles as a way to introduce the benefits of teamwork

WHAT YOU'LL NEED

- Two simple (60-100 piece) jigsaw puzzles

2 Introducing the Issue (20 minutes)

WHAT YOU'LL DO

- Discuss the benefits of, and barriers to teamwork
- Present a parable to reinforce the benefits of working together
- Complete the Unit Affirmation poster

WHAT YOU'LL NEED

- "Lefty: A Parable" Activity Sheet (page 119)
- Character signs
- Unit Affirmation poster

3 Searching the Scriptures (20 minutes)

WHAT YOU'LL DO

- Dramatize an interview to illustrate how we are better able to achieve our goals if we work together

WHAT YOU'LL NEED

- Bibles
- "Teamwork, The Secret of Champions" Activity Sheet (page 120)
- Bible covers from Lesson Three, drawing materials
- 9" x 12" pieces of colored paper-one piece for each student, with an equal number of pieces of each of these colors: red, orange, yellow, green, blue, violet

4 Living the Lesson (5-10 minutes)

WHAT YOU'LL DO

- Practice cooperating with others by playing a team game

WHAT YOU'LL NEED

- Paper clips—two for each student, half-sheet newspaper, stopwatch or clock with a second hand

✓ Lesson 4

Sports and Competition

✓ Setting the Stage (5-10 minutes)

As your students arrive today, get them working on the jigsaw puzzles you brought, creating two uneven teams. Depending on the size of your class, have one to three students work on one puzzle, and the rest of the students (at least three times as many) work on the second puzzle. Tell them this is a race, and the first ones to finish will be the winners. Obviously, the group with more students working on the puzzle will complete its puzzle first. When the first puzzle is completed, ask for volunteers to help the other group. **Why did the group with more of you working finish first?** (Working all together makes the task go more quickly.) **Did you notice any other benefits of working together?** Let kids share responses, keeping in mind that you will be further exploring this issue later in the lesson. **Today we are going to talk about what it means to be a team and how much more we can accomplish when we all work together.**

✓ Introducing the Issue (20 minutes)

When God created us, He made us with a need to have other people as a part of our lives. He doesn't intend for anyone to live or work all alone for an entire lifetime. What are some examples of things we cannot do without other people? (Be a family, have a conversation, play baseball.) **Many other things in life we could do alone, but they are usually more fun and easier when we do them with others. What are some examples of these things?** (Building something, playing certain games, taking a vacation.) **God's plan is for us to learn to live and work together. In other words, we need to learn about teamwork.**

Distribute copies of the activity sheet "Lefty: A Parable" (page 119). Choose seven volunteers to read this parable as a Reader's Drama. Distribute the signs to the characters to wear during the presentation. Position the players around the room in a way that depicts the feeling tone of the drama. For example, you could set Lefty off to one side to show his distance from the other parts of the body. You could have Heart sitting on the ground looking depressed or sad. Stomach could be munching on an apple. When the characters are ready, ask them to read through the play, putting a lot of feeling and expression into their parts. You may want to ask the characters to do a first run-through as a practice session in another area, to plan little staging touches, such as having everyone turn and stare at Stomach when he suggests going out for pizza. Take some time with this, and encourage the kids to really get into it. When

Sports and Competition

Lesson 4

they are ready, have the performers do their final presentation.

Why do you think Lefty wanted to leave the body? Allow for responses. Since the play doesn't really answer that question, kids can think of their own possibilities. **What would the results of Lefty's leaving be to the body?** (It would not function as well, Right foot would have to carry a heavier burden.) **What would the results of Lefty's leaving be to Lefty?** (He would have a tough time surviving by himself, he would be lonely.) **Lefty wanted to leave because at some point, he felt he was not important to the rest of the body. Have you ever felt like that?** Allow kids to talk about times when they may feel that their presence in their family, school class, team, or other setting was not needed, wanted, or appreciated.

Write two headings on the board: BENEFITS and BARRIERS. **Let's think about teamwork. What are some of the benefits of working together in teams?** As kids suggest ideas, list them on the board. Possibilities include: We are cared for and supported, a team can usually accomplish much more than anyone can alone, the job or game is more fun when we share it with others. **Even though we may know that teamwork is important, there are times when the teams of which we are a part do *not* function well together. What are some of the barriers to teams working together?** Possibilities might include: One person wants to be the boss and doesn't work with everyone else, a team member doesn't do his or her share of the work or game, poor communication, hurt feelings.

> **OPTIONAL:** Divide the class into two groups. Ask the first group to write an ending to the parable in which Lefty decides to leave the body, and the second group to write an ending in which he decides to stay in the body. Tell each group to write its endings in the same style as the parable; i.e., they will write out what Lefty says to announce his decision, and what several of the body parts say in response. As they work, circulate among the groups and give suggestions as needed. You can guide their thinking by asking some key questions; i.e., **if you were Lefty, what would you do?; what might Stomach say when he heard Lefty was leaving; Right Foot would probably have a lot to say, don't you think?** When they have completed their work, bring the class together again and ask for volunteers to read the play once again, this time adding one of the endings. When they are finished, ask for more volunteers to do it one more time, using the other ending.

Display the Unit Affirmation poster and read the Affirmation aloud together. Since this is the last week of the unit, review all the previous phrases, being sure kids understand each. Then have them think of a phrase to add for today.

115

Lesson 4

Sports and Competition

Possibilities might be: "when I work together with other teammates," or, "by being a team player." **Being a good team player is an important skill for many areas of our lives, including working together for God. Let's look at someone in the Bible who had a lot to say about Christians working together.**

✓ Searching the Scriptures (20 minutes)

Teamwork has benefits in many areas. The Apostle Paul had much to say about its value for Christians. Today we'll drop in on an interview with him about this important subject. Distribute copies of the activity sheet "Teamwork, The Secret of Champions" (page 120). Choose two readers to take the parts of Darbra Falters and Paul.

Now let's turn to Philippians 2:1-5 and read Paul's words for ourselves. Have students take turns reading this passage aloud. **In the first verse Paul lists some benefits of being Christians, being on the same team. What are they?** (Encouragement, Christ's comfort and love, fellowship with each other and the Spirit of God, tenderness—love for each other, compassion—sympathy.)

In the interview how did Paul say we can make great champions for God? (By cooperating with others and working together as a team to live the way Jesus did.) Read Philippians 2:3, 4. **Paul gives us a brief list of "do's" and "don'ts" about how to cooperate with each other. What are they?** You may want to list these on the board or a sheet of poster board so the class can see them better. Don'ts: do things out of selfish ambition or vain conceit, look after our own interests only. Do's: consider others better than ourselves, look after the interests of others.

In the interview, why did Darbra think people have trouble doing these things? (Because it's human nature to think of ourselves first.) **Do you think that's a good excuse? Why or why not?** One of the oldest and most used excuses for failing to obey God's laws is "I'm only human!" Point out that when we give our lives to Jesus, God's Holy Spirit comes to give us supernatural help to live the way God has planned for us.

Paul told Darbra that competition between Christians is harmful. What happens when they compete against each other? (They end up arguing, complaining, gossiping or putting each other down.) Many people are turned away from Jesus because they don't want to get involved with backbiting, quarreling churches. This kind of selfish, divisive behavior creates the wrong impression about God. It also earns a bad reputation for all Christians and makes it impossible for them to get anything accomplished.

Sports and Competition

Lesson 4

In the interview, Darbra felt that Timothy was more of a handicap than a help. How do we often treat people who don't quite measure up to our standards? (Many times we treat them like second-class citizens or unworthy of our love and friendship.) Point out that Paul lovingly provided comfort and help to Timothy. He patiently encouraged his good traits until Timothy became a valuable team worker in the Gospel. Ask someone to read aloud Philippians 2:20-22. **Why did Paul say he had no one else like Timothy?** (Timothy really cared about the welfare of others.) Point out that when Paul wasn't able to go himself, he trusted Timothy with some important jobs. Timothy repaid Paul by becoming like a son to him.

Why do you think God wants us to work and play together in unity? Let kids discuss this briefly based on what you have just studied, then have someone look up John 17:23b and read it aloud. **When Christians cooperate as a team others will be attracted to Jesus and know that we are united with Him in God's love.**

Have students say the Unit Verse, I Timothy 4:7b-8, together while running in place. Distribute the six colors of construction paper among students. Explain that they will work together as a team to help illustrate this Unit Verse. When you say a color, students with that color paper will hold it up and wave it. When you say rainbow all the kids will wave their papers.

Teamwork is like the many colors of a rainbow: red, orange yellow, green, blue, indigo and violet. If green thinks it has the right to overpower orange, the rainbow isn't what it should be. If the whole rainbow is only red how can it be what God intended? If the only color were blue, how could the rainbow show up in the sky? If yellow decides it doesn't show up as much as violet, does that mean it isn't part of the rainbow? God placed all the colors, red, orange, yellow, green, blue, violet, in the rainbow because He wanted them that way. We are all special members of God's team, His rainbow, and by working together we can reach the goals He has for us.

Distribute the Bible covers used in the previous lessons. Write this statement on the board and have students complete it: "Training yourself in teamwork for God has value because . . . ?" Illustrations can be added as time allows.

✓ Living the Lesson (5-10 minutes)

Now that we've had a chance to see how Paul and Timothy worked together, let's try it out by playing a game that requires teamwork.

TUBE TEAMWORK: Clear an open space in the room. Ask everyone to stand in a circle. Give players two paper clips each. Have players take the pieces of construction paper they used for the rainbow reading and roll them into

Lesson 4

Sports and Competition

twelve-inch tubes with about a one-inch overlap. Fasten the ends of each tube with paper clips. Crush a piece of newspaper into a ball small enough to pass through these tubes. Players hold their tubes end-to-end to create one large circular tube. Choose one person to be Starter. Drop the paper ball into the end of the starter's tube. Players must pass the ball by shaking it from one tube to the next. If the ball falls on the floor, it can be picked up and returned to the tube. Players can pass the ball only from tube to tube without touching the newspaper ball. When the ball gets back to the Starter, tube players reverse the direction of the circle. When the paper ball returns to the Starter again, the game is completed. You may want to play against the clock and see how long it takes to pass the ball around the circle. Then try to beat that time when you go the opposite direction. Teamwork is essential and everybody wins.

Have the students sit in the circle after the game and talk about their experience. **How did playing together make you feel? How is what you've just done like Paul and Timothy? What can you learn from this? What will you do differently because you've worked together today?**

We are better able to achieve our goals when we work together with others. Have students join hands and close their eyes while you pray thanking God for each student in your class, each one a special member of God's team.

Lefty: A Parable

Characters: Right foot, left foot, leg, arm, hand, heart, and stomach.

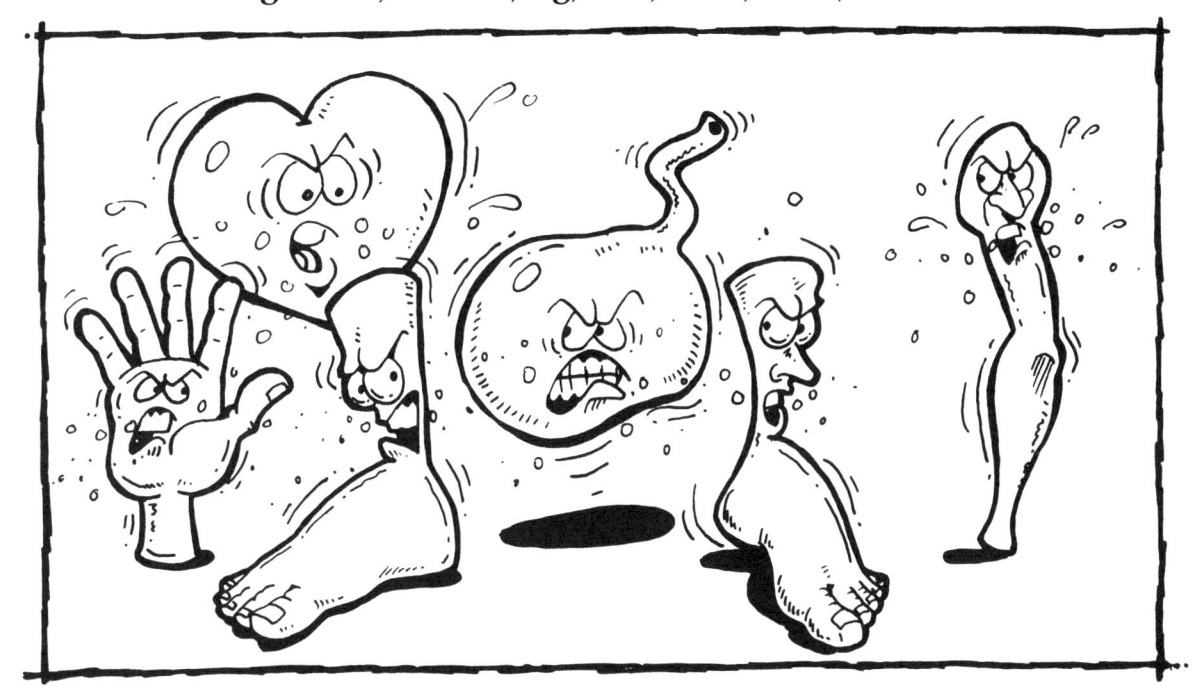

LEFT FOOT: I'm sorry, but my mind is made up.
HEART: But you can't leave the body! How will we get along without you?
RIGHT FOOT: Yeah, Lefty! Do you realize what happens if you leave? I have to pick up the slack and carry your load!
LEFTY: Look, I'm sorry you are all upset. But you'll get along just fine without me! You don't need me to keep going. You'll probably never even know I'm gone. I'm just not that important to this body. Not like stomach over there.
STOMACH: Yeah, guess I am the star player here. This body would starve to death if it weren't for me!
HAND: Oh yeah? Well how do you think you would function if Arm and I just left, huh? Don't forget, we're the ones who get the food to you in the first place! You'd be nowhere without us!
ARM: Look, Lefty, we are all important to this body! Where would hand be without me? And where would I be without hand? Just a useless stump!
HEART: Besides, we love you! Maybe we don't always show it, but we really do love you!
RIGHT FOOT: Look, buddy, I need you! I can't do all the walking by myself. We're a team, remember?
LEG: And don't forget about me! I'm a part of this team, too. Without you, I can't get anywhere!
STOMACH: Wait a minute! I got it! Let's all go out for pizza! Pizza fixes everything!
LEFTY: Hey, back off, will ya? You make it sound as if everything will fall apart if I leave! I hardly think I'm that important!
HAND: Oh, we'd survive without you. But we wouldn't work as well together. After all this time, don't you realize that our body needs all of us to work together?
ARM: Come on, Lefty! Stay with us! What do you say?
LEFTY: Well . . . .

Activity Sheet by Linda Kondracki © 1991 David C. Cook Publishing Co. Permission granted to reproduce for classroom use only.

✓ Teamwork, The Secret of Champions

Darbra Falters: Hello, I'm Darbra Falters. We're here today to talk to Paul, who is known for attracting thousands of people to Jesus throughout the world. What is the secret of your success?
Paul: Teamwork, Darbra. People working together on God's team.
Darbra: How does this work?
Paul: Team members work together and show a real interest in other people. In some churches we have people from many different backgrounds. Working towards the same goal isn't always easy. Competition among ourselves is harmful.
Darbra: Isn't it just human nature to think of ourselves first and be competitive? How can you say it's harmful?
Paul: When Christians argue, complain, and use put-downs, it hurts all of us. We need to humbly put others first in order to carry out God's plan for us.
Darbra: In saying we need to be humble are you saying that we should put ourselves down? Won't that create a poor self-image?
Paul: No. We're humble because we're all sinners. Christians are just sinners who are saved by God's undeserved love and kindness. Because we love and trust Jesus, God has forgiven us. That gives us true worth.
Darbra: Then how can they consider others better than themselves?
Paul: They can care about the problems of others as if they were their own. They can work together to tell people about Jesus and share God's love with them.
Darbra: You have a helper named Timothy, don't you, Paul? What is his part in all this?
Paul: He is a special member of God's team. He has been just like a son to me.
Darbra: Tell us something about him.
Paul: He comes from a mixed cultural background. Timothy is young, shy, and rather sickly. Sometimes he needs encouragement.
Darbra: It sounds as if he is more of a handicap than a help.
Paul: Oh, no. I have no one else like Timothy. Most people only think about themselves, but not Timothy. He really cares about others. Sometimes I send him on important errands because I know I can trust him to care for others like Jesus did. He's a valuable member of God's team.
Darbra: Then you would say that the secret that makes great champions for God is...
Paul: Teamwork, Darbra. People working together to glorify God.

Activity Sheet by Bev Gundersen © 1991 David C. Cook Publishing Co. Permission granted to reproduce for classroom use only.

Junior Electives

Service Projects for Sports and Competition

In addition to the projects listed in these lessons your class or church can also serve in the following ways:

✓ 1. Hold a "Teamwork Olympics" where all the games are based on cooperation and everyone is a winner. Teams can compete against the clock or try to better their own records.

✓ 2. Use your bodies and minds to work together on a project that will benefit your church or school such as yard or playground beautification.

✓ 3. Give a free car wash as a gesture of cooperation for Christ.

✓ 4. Plan and help set up a sports program for homeless children or those of migrant workers. Use games and exercises that emphasize teamwork and cooperation. Be sure to model good attitudes of winners and losers.

✓ 5. Design an activity program for a nursing home or the developmentally or physically handicapped. Take into account the special needs of residents and plan suitable games.

✓ 6. Go as a group to play against an institutional team. They will welcome playing somebody new for a change and will feel part of the community again.

✓ 7. Volunteer to help out with the recreation time for a VBS, Day Camp, or Summer Ministry program.